Remembering Qualities of Your Soul:

Joyfully Living your Godself

Paul L. Hannah M.D.
Master Teacher Healer

Remembering Qualities of Your Soul: Joyfully Living your Godself

Published by Mason Works Press; Boulder, Colorado.

For information, please contact Kathy Mason, Publisher,
at kathy@masonworksmarketing.com,
or write to Mason Works Press, 6525 Gunpark Dr. #370-426,
Boulder, CO 80301.

Disclaimer: While the publisher and author have used their best efforts in preparing this book, they make no representations or warranties with respect to its accuracy or completeness. In addition, this book contains no legal or medical advice; please consult a licensed professional if appropriate.

Cover and Interior Design by Kathy Mason and Maryann Sperry
Cover photo by NASA

ISBN: 978-0-9983209-2-2 (Softcover)

First Edition

Library of Congress Control Number: On file

Published in the United States of America

Printed in the United States of America

"For those people seeking guidance on the spiritual path, Dr. Hannah's book is both a metaphorical map and compass to help you return home again. Keen sights, wonderful affirmations and ageless wisdom come together in an alchemy of inspiration that makes this a timeless resource for spiritual growth."

Brian Luke Seaward, Ph.D., author of the bestselling book, *Stand Like Mountain, Flow Like Water* and *Stressed Is Desserts Spelled Backward*

"As a Radical Mindfulness expert, I can easily identify when other Masters share life's Truth. Dr. Paul Hannah's new book, Remembering Qualities of Your Soul: Joyfully Living Your Godself *provides so many verities that can quickly transform people to a remarkable life through spiritual transformation."*

Daniel Gutierrez, author of *Radical Mindfulness*

"Dr. Hannah's book is all about energy: our energetic essence, the energetic essence of the universe, and how to get them in sync. For him that means raising the vibrational level and quality of our soul essence energy to match and resonate with the infinite, quantum energy of all that is. As he clearly explains, our soul is already 'wired' to do that, but life's distractions, distortions, and detractors have disrupted and suppressed that connection. So Dr. Hannah offers us several concrete ways to reconnect and realign those energies and truly manifest the qualities that our soul is there to express. That makes this book an invaluable guide to doing what its subtitle promises: Joyfully Living Your Godself. *Wow, what an opportunity! Making this book a must-read, more than once for sure."*

Dr. William Spady, New Paradigm Network, Leadership and OBE Expert

"*In* Remembering Qualities of Your Soul: Joyfully Living Your Godself, *Paul Hannah, M.D., offers us the freedom and love needed to ascend to a higher level of energy and powerful living. My work centers around creatively living in the possibility space, and through Paul's guidance, you too can discover ways to connect to the highest, creative expression of yourself. These universal truths will change your life.*"

Elsie Ritzenhein, Ed. Sp. CEO, Inspiring Creative Women. Author of *Awakening Your Creative Voice/Women in a World of Possibilities.* Co-author of *Generative Leadership/Shaping New Futures for Today's Schools.*

"*In* Remembering Qualities of Your Soul: Joyfully Living Your Godself, *Dr. Paul L Hannah reminds us all that we are filled with light and one with the Creator/Source Energy. He thoughtfully and generously shares his wisdom, offers tools, affirmations and explains Laws of The Universe that help the reader live a life in the light. Dr. Paul L Hannah reminds us that it is possible to live a life filled with awakened love, courage, compassion, beauty, faith and breath. A life of oneness with the Creator/Source.* Remembering Qualities of Your Soul: Joyfully Living Your Godself *is a beautifully written, inspirational book worth reading.*"

America Martinez, International Intuitive Consultant

"*At a time when humanity needs to urgently wake up to its potential to live in harmony and with a higher consciousness that can benefit all, Dr. Hannah offers an important path of insight and awakening that will help you understand yourself, your power and your important role in the evolution of energy and wholeness for all. Both metaphysically rich and personally practical, this is a wonderful guide for the soul and the mastery of subtle energy."*

Dr. Jonathan Ellerby, two-time bestselling author of *Return to the Sacred*

"Paul has written an amazing guide to higher frequency living with his book Remembering Qualities of Your Soul. *I will recommend this book to all my clients to help them better understand how to maintain higher frequencies to have a more powerful, fulfilling life. This is book is packed with important truths for successfully living your soul purpose and utilizing your Divine gifts as God in human form."*

Cindy Bentley, International Energy Practitioner, author of *Celestial Being: How to Shift to Fifth Dimensional Living* www.DNAreconnection.com

"As we shift towards a life filled with unconditional love and gratitude, we resonate a field of healing rainbow light. I'm hopeful that readers of Dr. Hannah's inspiring book, Remembering Qualities of Your Soul *will re-kindle this light within their hearts and awaken others to return towards oneness and love for one another."*

Fred Grover Jr. M.D. Integrative Medicine physician and author of *Spiritual Genomics* and *Awakening Gaia.*

"*Dr. Hannah has written such a beautiful and empowering book that is full of Divine Light, Love and Wisdom. The book is concise but yet contains many great spiritual teachings and good information on health and wellness. I thoroughly enjoyed this book and would highly recommend it to those who are seekers and on a journey to their own awakening. I especially love the simple but powerful affirmations.*

Dr. Hannah is truly a great teacher, master and enlightened being. We are so fortunate to get the best of both world's wisdom through his incredible and extensive background in Western Medicine, Qi Gong, Martial Arts and spirituality. I loved this book and will definitely read it again!"

Blake Sinclair, author of *Dare to Imagine, Beyond Imagination, A New Beginning*, blogger, founder of U.U.M.M. meditation system, founder of I AM Wellness Method, Mystic, Life Coach and Wellness Optimizer, and Licensed Occupational Therapist

"Remembering Qualities of Your Soul *by Paul Hannah, M.D. takes the reader through profound and transcendent principles to guide your life to higher soul awareness, which he calls your Godself. As another MD who has expanded my practice to offer non-traditional western medicine for higher spiritual healing, I recommend this book as a powerful guide to holistic wellness.*"

Mani Saint-Victor, M.D., bestselling author of *Thinking About Quitting Medicine*

SPECIAL ACKNOWLEDGMENTS

Earten Hannah (Grandfather)

Dorothy Hannah Gladney (Mother)

Dr. David M. Berry – Metaphysical Teacher and Spiritual Earth Father

June May Kortum of The Gathering Lighthouse, Lisle, IL

Sechul Kim – Teacher

Jeung San Do – Meditation Center

DEDICATION

This book is dedicated to my Ancestors, the Love Warriors, the Truth Seekers, my Teachers and Students, Friends, Family, and all the Light Workers of future generations.

TABLE OF CONTENTS

INTRODUCTION

I am grateful that you have a magnetic connection to this book. There is a vibrational frequency attraction that aligns with your deep inner urge to REMEMBER Qualities of your Soul. There is an energetic shift on planet earth that is causing tremendous destabilization and imbalances mentally, emotionally, physically and spiritually. There is also an increase in the polarization and separation of countries, religions and races.

As this toxic energy continues to rise, each person will challenge themselves to seek ways to maintain balance. One must take total responsibility for their thoughts, breathing and actions to maintain a state of radiant, joyful balance. We are challenged to look internally for our methods of raising our awareness, concentration and vibrational energetic frequency. We are made of energy. Energy can't be destroyed. It can only be transformed. Every human being is responsible for transforming their energy. There are collective thoughts/ consensus that someone other than themselves is responsible for their happiness, health, freedom and wealth. The more one looks outside of themselves and blames their destabilization and lack of balance on someone else, the worse they become.

This imbalance is associated with lack of appreciation and abuse of the physical body by; eating, drinking, and sleeping unhealthily, all of which has a low vibrational thought frequency. This attracts more of the same low energetic thought frequency and a life of misery, anxiety, depression, energetic poverty, and loneliness. I had these thoughts, feelings and habits. Then I had an awakening that I was the creator of my world. It was up to me to take total responsibility for my feelings, thoughts, behaviors and actions. There are no victims, just volunteers. Every human being/soul has the FREE WILL to choose and be responsible for their thinking feeling and actions.

Are you responding from a reactive mode or a joyfully being responsible for your thinking, feeling, or behavior?

I am writing this book because of the Love Energy Healing flowing in through me to the world. There is a strong inner urge to transmit love, harmony and truth with every breath I take.

Imagine that all the world's problems could be resolved by inhaling love and exhaling harmony, and how this could raise the consciousness and vibrational frequency. Join me in imagining 8 billion people on earth inhaling love and exhaling harmony; which would raise the vibrational frequency of the Earth. This will be a moment of Joyful Universal Oneness. Thank you for taking this journey with me, with this powerful process.

As a Master Teacher Healer of energies that awakens and empowers, I became aware of LOVE POWER's transforming effect on Energy. This book is written with the intention to stimulate you to Remember Qualities of Your Soul (Godself).

The soul energy is in your unique individualized aspect of Source and called by many names in many religions. Regardless of the various religions or beliefs there is one underlying common denominator LOVE.

Love source energy is embedded in our spiritual DNA, which means that we are Individualized Aspects of the Source (God). This profound realization motivates me to live with CONFIDENCE, COURAGE, and CREATIVITY with tremendous will power being my Godself. This source/soul energy is available to everyone, regardless of the way they were raised, wealth, physical or mental status. It is available to be used to create anything that one desires with deserving.

I am inviting you to go on an inner journey with me to a high radiant energy, self-mastery and transformation. This journey will entail imagination, visualization, with divine realization of your soul source Oneness. This journey will assist you to becoming aware of your individualized creative source energy where everything exists. There are no limits, except in your mind.

As you wake up and become the creator of all of your dreams, aware of your unlimited potential of bliss and abundance and one with source, it raises your vibrational frequencies that are aligned with joyfulness, abundance, happiness, and vibrant health. Imagination plays a huge role in creating your dreams. The powerful utilization of imagination was taught by the Ancient Master Teachers that imagination can expand one's consciousness. One of the most famous contemporary energy masters, Physicist, Albert Einstein; who stated that *'Imagination was one of the greatest discoveries of the 21st century.'*

REMEMBERING QUALITIES OF YOUR SOUL

Consciousness is the doorway to Knowledge. Knowledge is the doorway to Wisdom. Wisdom is the doorway to Freedom.

As we go through this process of the qualities of the soul, you will learn how to transform toxic energy. The key lesson is that you have to practice with sincerity, burning desire, deserving, discipline, detachment and determination to change your life and connect with your soul. With these practices, you will develop more confidence with clarity and creativity.

Discovering Qualities of your Soul:

Inside this book, we will explore ways of remembering your divine self. To have a high quality of living, you have to align with qualities of your soul/Godself. You are the only person that can do it for yourself. It is to <u>EMBRACE THE REALITY THAT YOUR ARE YOUR OWN</u> Guru, Teacher, and Master Healer. I am a reflector and catalyst for you to Remember Your Soul/Godself Qualities.

I will guide you through fundamental *Soul Qualities* to enable you to align yourself with your Soul/Godself. This new awakened consciousness will give you more love, gratitude, joy, freedom and be of service of love vibration on planet earth.

PART 1

WAKE UP

A re you ready to awaken to your GodSelf?

A fundamental truth is that we are one with the divine source. We are Godman and Goddess, as stated in the hermetic philosophy, *'As above, so below.'* Stated another way we all have the spiritual DNA from the creator. I am a catalyst to help you to remember your divine self. Waking up to that divine self is different for each person.

My wake-up call to dwell deeper in remembering my divine soul source was stimulated by frustration, limitations, observing rampant ignorance, greed, anger and the delusion of separatism. There was a deeper stimulation to transform my level of consciousness. That level presented by the realization that there is one energy, one love, one breath.

Unconditional love creates more light and living from love and light I shine bright in this dark earthly plight. PLH

Constant cultivation of love and light create a heart frequency of coherence, connection, caring and compassion. And this frequency not only raises one's vibration, it expands exponentially.

As my frequency expanded, I became more of an observer and onlooker. I have always been an observer since childhood, observing people and the world around me. I became more awake and aware as I observed my own feelings, thoughts and beliefs that was creating my reality. I also become aware that the universal laws were unlimited, and accessible to all who apply the conscious laws of creating.

Wake up to universal truths

Universal laws are unbiased they are beyond the manipulation and alteration of human beings. The law is precise, and energy is returned back to you based upon beliefs, thoughts and actions. Ignorance of the laws does not excuse the negative energetic effects of your thinking and actions. I frequently encounter people stating that they didn't know something they did and are hoping and expecting to be forgiven for their actions.
Wake up and realize that your THOUGHTS ARE ENERGY. The big question is:

WHAT ARE YOU THINKING?

BE AWARE OF YOUR THOUGHTS because they CREATE YOUR REALITY.

Utilizing the universal laws are vital for living your Godself. Godself is source energy that is one with the Creator. Love is the interconnecting energy of your Godself and Source Energy / Creator.

CHAPTER 1

DIVINE AWAKENING

Awakening is a dynamic conscious energetic process that connects one to Creator Soul Energy and Eternal Soul Inheritance.

What are some stimuli for Awakening?

There is an inner feeling and curiosity of many questions: Why am I here? What is my purpose for being born in this time on planet earth? Who am I? What else exists beyond this physical life? What is heaven? Often these questions get pushed to the side because of one's busy lifestyle.

There are three essential events that stimulate awakening:

I

The malalignment of your mental, emotional, intellectual and physical body with Soul will create pain. Pain of any type is a powerful stimulus for Awakening. Having survived a near death episode, be it from terminal cancer, infection or some other stimulus.

II

Holding a thought about awakening will attract one to a person, institute, group, media or book that will stimuli awakening. It is a universal, energetic law that energy of the same vibrational frequency attracts. This much thought brings one clarity and momentum to learn and remember more of one's Soul Qualities.

III

Some people are born with a gift of feeling, seeing, hearing, and feeling energy incarnate. They are mediums. All psychics are not mediums, but all mediums are psychics. Having this gift can increase the awakening to higher dimensions.

Who Benefits from Ignorance?

Major industries benefit from ignorance of the masses of people because it creates and maintains a constant cash flow. Ignorance and dependence are extremely lucrative. Look at the medical, legal, healers of all types, social services, educators, politicians, plumbers, and carpenters who all make money from ignorance. I teach that people and corporations spend money for convenience and ignorance. For example, I take my car to a mechanic for repair, or call a plumber to fix the pipes because I am ignorant of how to repair it myself. Therefore, I pay for ignorance.

Every soul that reincarnates on earth has one more gift/intent and deserves compensation. It is up to the individual to use their gift with empathy or be a bully and abuse, manipulate to perpetuate ignorance and dependence.

When one utilizes their gift selfishly, it reflects energy with a negative return. They become more ignorant than the people that foster dependence and ignorance because of universal energetic violation.

Remember whatever you do you do it to yourself.

You reap what you sow.

Positively using one's gift or talent is to have gratitude for your gift. Utilize it to awaken and raise the vibrational frequency of the person, patient, client, or customer, whereas they become more elevated. Practice the method and tap into the unlimited flow of abundance with people to serve.

Sharing with gratitude and unconditional love has a profound effect of raising individual, institution and planet vibrational frequencies.

Now you know the law of energetic flow and decide which way <u>you decide</u> to flow. It is your choice.

Love is the new currency.

How much unconditional love have you invested in yourself, others and the planet?

AFFIRMATION

I am awakening my Soul's Love and Light shining bright for humanity's delight to be bright. Join me if you might.

CHAPTER 2

SOUL PURPOSE

In essence, one's soul purpose is to remember that their divine DNA is one with the Creator/Source Energy. Ancient Hermetic philosophy states, "As above, so below". This is a great metaphor, meaning that we have the inner source within to accept our divine self. Every soul is endowed with gifts and talents. Proper alignment and cultivating one's gifts and talents, creates inner peace, harmony, radiant health, abundance prosperity motivated by unconditional love. The unconditional love emits a vibrational frequency of compassionate service to humanity. Therefore, increasing love energy to people, places, animals, and to Mother Earth.

As the soul is reincarnated into a family, race, social economic status which provides it with the maximum opportunities on the earth planc. It is important to realize that the soul is housed by the physical body. The physical body is dominated by ego. It is important to distinguish or become aware of the limited ego energy from the unlimited soul energy. The ego is dominated by the illusion of separatism, doubt, fear, anger, greed and ignorance. This material world that we live in constantly feeds and stimulates the ego which causes one to look outside of themselves for peace, and satisfaction. As we live life we encounter challenges: emotional, pain, stress, frustration, and some hardships that become motivation for one to look within. As we look deeper inside, we encounter our divine eternal qualities. The earth plane/school is where we have the golden opportunity to become conscious of our inner divinity and live our joyful Godself.

Every soul is in earth school and every situation offers an opportunity to learn. We have a choice to learn, deny or resist. To deny or resist is an ineffective way of dealing with conflicts, hardships and disappointments. An example is the educational system: you must pass each grade to graduate, if you are oppositional, resist or deny, you fail to graduate. As an adult in a relationship, you have to know the reason and how you played a part of the success or failure of the relationship. Everything that happens to us we co-created. We must be honest with ourselves about the role we played. What did I do, how can I make this (negative) experience positive for me? Eliminate blaming and flip it to claiming your inner divinity.

As we develop the habit of optimism, we transform all alleged setbacks, ups and downs as an opportunity to graduate from your situation. Once you graduate, you graduate. Sometimes we prolong this graduation because of our attachments. Delaying graduation from relationships, jobs, family is a form of inner stagnation. Delaying graduation from a job, education, relationship, or family is a confirmation that you are coming from the ego. There is a lack of trust in one's divine self, knowing that all is well, and everything happens for the best.

Some relationships last a lifetime, and some don't. There is no right or wrong about it. It is what it is. There is no reason to compare yourself to your friend and family as they have their own soul lesson. You might have seen it within yourself despite liking or loving someone that it is time for graduation. Are you staying because of comfort and fear, being needed or afraid to hurt someone's feelings? Your decision must be based on the highest good, truth and unconditional love.

Earth Plane Lessons

The question is:

WHAT IS THE PROCESS OF MAXIMIZING OUR LESSONS ON THE EARTH PLANE?

Clarity

One must be clear about developing their soul purpose. When you have clarity, you can focus your energy. Your clear persistent thought process expands energy and maximizes accomplishing your goal. Clarity in this material world can be challenging. It takes courage, faith and trust to maintain focus in this high-tech world. Clarity will help you to let go of distractions impeding living your soul purpose.

Courage

Courage is the inner strength to transcend popular beliefs, family culture or tribal consciousness. Your soul connection is through the continual cultivation of courage to be your divine self. Remember, "To Thy own self be true."

The world depends on people like us, to have the courage to stand up, while being compassionate, non-judgmental, strong, creative, and consistent on your path.

Be aware and have the courage to stand in your light, intentionally shining brightly.

Confidence

Confidence is a core quality that empowers you to accomplish every goal that you desire. It is a knowing that you are a part of the Creator/the grand ultimate source energy. There are no limitations except in your mind which may not feel worthy by and having an attitude of wanting. There is a confusion between want and desire, and a lot of frustration about not getting what one desires because there is a big difference between the energy of wanting and the energy of desire. Wanting is associated with lack and lack is associated with unworthiness, which is a negative repulsive energy. You can never get what you desire with an attitude of wanting.

Another feature of confidence that I particularly like is when you have the energy and confidence to transcend tribal consciousness, the well-established social system and the opinion of others.

Conscious Connection

Having an ever-present state of consciousness enhances one's energy of manifesting through effortless radiant energy. Your life will flow in a joyful harmonic way.

It is my intention that this book will put you in touch with the spiritual resources that God/source energy has placed inside of all of us. The ability to transmit loving energy, to shine with abundance, to connect someone with their inner healing power, these are eternal gifts from the creator. They cannot be owned by any person or individual ego, they can only be honored and revealed.

Honoring these gifts happens naturally when we spend time with ourselves, free of distractions, with our attention focused inside. Quality time with oneself helps us to discover who we really are, it helps us to feel the full extent of our inner wealth. Getting to know who you are means communicating with the indwelling God/source energy, with the part of you that is in tune with the source of all life.

AFFIRMATION

I am living my soul purpose and eagerly serving
humanity with my gifts.

.

CHAPTER 3

RESPONSIBILITY

Responsibility on the path to remembering your soul quality is owning your feelings, beliefs and actions. As one's consciousness and heart of love frequency expands there is no blaming, or victims invested in gossip, because you understand that every thought, feeling and beliefs have their own vibrational frequency. Those frequencies that radiate back to you are whatever frequency you send out.

I became responsible at an early age, getting up at dawn, to feed the animals, eat breakfast and get to the school bus by 6am. I grew up with a clear expectation, knowing I fulfilled what I was capable of doing; that created a strong foundation of being responsible.

External physical life begins when the umbilical cord is cut between the mother and the baby. It begins with inhalation-the breath of life. The mother cannot breathe life or do the bodily expression for the baby. It is the responsibility of the baby to do this on its own.

There is a positive correlation with teaching and expecting everyone to be responsible for themselves. Doing for others what they can do for themselves, creates dependency, resentment, and lack of appreciation towards the individual who is "over doing". This is demonstrated by patients who give the responsibility of their health to physicians, energy healers, religious leaders, Qi Gong and Reiki masters, psychologists, social workers and therapists. Often, they look for someone else to solve their problems by abdicating their own internal responsibility. My purpose of sharing this is to remind you that everyone has the divine responsibility and ability to activate the inner healer and guru for themselves.

Learning to have inner trust, knowing that you are deserving and connected to your Godself, enhances your responsibility of creating radiant health, happiness, joy, peace and abundance. As we advance deeper on the inner path, we develop more confidence. When we know that we are one with the source energy plus surrounded by angelic forces and ancestors that are readily available for our assistance, we can trust that we are divinely supported. Before you ask, make sure you honestly did all you can before you can ask for more support. The angels and ancestors will only help if you ask- they will not interfere without your permission.

There are three criteria for enhancing your responsibility:

I

Have an attitude of joyfulness, while being non-judgmental in your thinking, beliefs, feeling and actions.

No individual is perfect in the physical body, we reincarnated for our soul to learn lessons from our earthly experience. When these lessons are painful or frustrating, it is an indication of malalignment with unconditional love and unconditional truth. As you align to self-love/your GodSelf, unconditional love and universal truth will transform fear, attachments, greed, victimization, and toxic beliefs. Your frequency raises to create a radiant life.

II

Have a burning desire to create and be responsible for your own happiness and individuality.

No one can make nor are they responsible for your happiness, that is a total individual responsibility. It can take 2 people to experience joy, 2 people can have conflict, but there is only one person who is responsible for their own happiness. When you encounter people who you find irritating, frustrating, or boring just remember they are reflecting you because they are things you haven't resolved yet.

They become your reflective mirror. In your individuality you will be challenged by your degree of attachment with your family, race, gender, religious and political beliefs which may not be consistent with your true individuality. When you deny who you are and what you are for the sake of others you will never reach your maximum potential, happiness, or joy because you are living a sense of denial and irresponsibility.

Remembering and living your true individuality requires you having courage, discipline and detachment to transcend anything, anybody and any situation that is impeding or suppressing your unique individuality. Recognize that your unique individuality fully expressed is a part of the planetary awakening consciousness that is expanding purification, unification and harmonization So be who you are and walk in your love light and shine bright.

III

Develop an attitude of gratitude for all the events in your life.

Especially with adversity and emotional pain, this is a golden opportunity to remember the vastness of your divine creativity. Gratitude has the ability to neutralize and transform disharmonious energies from people, places and things to a radiant oneness. There is no separatism or dualities except in our mind, because in the ultimate truth there is one energy, one love, one breath with many variations that appear to be different. It is like the sun, that has many rays but comes from one source.

Responsibility is empowering and a catalyst that allows you to open to the universe for things to flow freely. I encourage you to take responsibility for everything in your life and have the confidence for creating your life platform. Develop relationships, family, friends, lifestyle, utilizing your gifts to serve the planet in terms of health, happiness and prosperity.

"There are no victims, only volunteers" PLH

AFFIRMATION

I am totally responsible for my thoughts, beliefs, feelings, health, happiness and wealth.

CHAPTER 4

POWER OF THOUGHT/LAW OF ENERGY

**Thought is an energetic principle that makes
the invisible visible**

Being aware and controlling one's thoughts is essential for cultivating and remembering one's soul qualities. I am inspired to share this awareness about consciousness, thought and energy.

Conscious thought has two dominant features:

1. Intensity - Associated with the focus of the thought
2. Vibration - Associated with the frequency of the thought

Intensity and frequency have magnetic features that attract equal energetic frequency. Have you noticed how Positive people attract Positive people and Negative people attract Negative people? This is Universal Law.

Another Universal Law is Energy can't be destroyed it can only be transformed.

That is why it is so important to be aware of your thoughts by having an ever-present state of consciousness. Your conscious or unconscious thoughts create your reality.

> *"Everything that happens in all material, living, mental or even spiritual processes involves the transformation of energy... Every thought, every sensation, every emotion is produced by energy exchanges."* J.G. Bennett

On the path to remembering the qualities of the soul, one must be aware of utilizing FREE WILL and DIVINE CHOICE.

There are massive new waves of energy showering the atmosphere of planet earth as evidenced by increased tsunamis, earthquakes, and weather changes. These energy waves have a profound effect on people's consciousness and focus. It is very difficult to have clarity of thought which leads to frustration, depression, confusion, anxiety and anger.

It has become very important to have clarity of thought!

You should ask yourself, WHAT ARE YOU THINKING? Are your happy with what you see? Is it beautiful or is it ugly?

Whatever it is, you created it.

It was your thought creation. The universe always gives you your predominant thought. When your thoughts don't manifest your desire, it causes a problem.

This is solved by applying three words, which includes:

WHAT, WHEN AND HOW

I intentionally didn't use WHY. (Because WHY is judgmental and critical.)

To have crystal-clear thought processes, begin with your WHAT (confidence) your WHEN (courage) and your HOW (which utilizes creativity and help from one's ancestors, angel and celestial team). Using this method will increase the intensity and vibrational frequency to magnify your power.

> *"As you change your thinking to higher vibrational thoughts, you are contributing to the efforts."* Sananda and the Beings of Light

Effort leads to a conscious energetic thought expanding harmonious frequency in one's life, radiant health, joyful relationships, peace, beauty, compassion and more service to humanity and planet earth.

Thought Is So Powerful

Whatever you do, you do to yourself. Our thoughts create our lives, bodies, and states of being. Everyone is responsible for their own journey, and we are all interconnected. As we move from Ego to Soul to GodSelf, we become aware that we are responsible to feed ourselves internally with loving thoughts that connect to love vibrations of like-minded people throughout the planet.

Energy Pathways Truths

- Human energy is cultivated by the quality of our thought, breath, water, food, sun, and environment.

- Energy begets energy, whereas the more I help others, the more others help me.

- Everything returns to the source, whatever you send out comes back to you.

By moving from REACTION, which causes inner stress and depletes your energy to RESPONSE, to consciousness and deliberation, you are positioned to stay in the positive and to deal with what it is. This helps us to take responsibility. To progress we must own our current state, alongside the process of reaching our desired state. Any kind of growth requires that we get out of our comfort zones.

If you have anger you have to release it and move on.

Some say, "you cannot afford to be angry for more than 20 seconds" because of the physical damage it can do to your body. Studies show that sustained anger and stress have a negative impact.

Qi Gong and intentional breathing help calm us down and control anger. Controlling anger with conscious breathing decreases the toxic release of cortisol; which effects physical, mental, emotional, intellectual, and spiritual increases your frequency to a higher vibration.

If you believe and understand that whatever you do, you do to yourself, you will be spiraling up your energy closer to your Godself. The more we trust this the more we can follow it.

AFFIRMATION

I have clear thoughts of Love and Light
Shining Bright.

PART 2

GET UP

The process of getting up is having a burning desire, inner knowing and remembering that the soul has a higher vibrational frequency and dimension. This expands one's conscious connection and allows one's unique individualized divine being to be expressed. Expressing one's divine uniqueness individuality transcends the limited linear ego (edging God out) to a soul unlimited vibrational frequency. Expressing one's soul unique energy frequency, involves having receptivity to one's higher self, ancestors, angels and guides.

Receptivity and trust are needed to reach higher frequency to stimulate remembering your divine soul qualities. Receptivity is the prerequisite for the continuation of humans, mammals, flowers, fruit and vegetative life. One must have an empty mind/cup of receptivity to receive higher knowledge, love and wisdom.

It may be difficult for some individuals who identify with their superb IQ, Religious dogma, degrees or credentials to be receptive. Practicing gratitude is a powerful method of neutralizing arrogant and elitist mentalities. We must always be an onlooker of our mentality, behaviors. judgment and intellectual bullying that feeds one's insecurities.

Are you a bully, hiding?

Gratitude is a soul quality that stands alone and allows one to appreciate every person encountered on a daily basis. It offers a golden opportunity to be receptive to inner growth, because each individual is a reflective mirror to confirm, inspire, educate, and clarify our inner qualities. Practicing gratitude cultivates and expands one's energy to live one's life purpose. Clarity of purpose enhances 'divine will' to stay on the inner journey to live ones joyful Godself.

CHAPTER 5

RECEPTIVITY

Developing Divine Receptivity

Receptivity is a powerful energetic principle that is needed for the continuation of humans, plants and flowers on planet earth. Relaxation is necessary for the impregnation of planting seeds, flowers and also being able to receive truth and universal laws. For example, the egg must be receptive to the sperm to ensure fertilization. And every gardener and farmer know that the soil must toiled which is a form of relaxation before the seeds are planted.

A Master Teacher has compassion and patience for the student to become receptive. A Master Teacher is motivated by love, and source energy and NEVER teaches before the student is receptive. This would be a violation of the Spiritual Law to force beyond receptivity. That impatience is associated with egotistical teaching and is not based on patience or compassion. On the quest for remembering the qualities of the soul, one needs to have a receptive mind and an empty cup to receive universal truth and wisdom. As you can see relaxation and humility enhances receptivity.

What is the process of developing Divine receptivity?

I am defining DIVINE RECEPTIVITY as an eagerness to transcend one's present limited knowledge.

Having knowledge cultivates or enhances your victorious mindset because of when you are ignorant of something you become a victim of the situation. And being ignorant is a serious liability to one's health, happiness, prosperity, success of your true self.

BE IN THE KNOW SO YOU CAN FLOW YOUR DIVINE GLOW.

In contrast, one can choose to follow the ego which limits their energy flow, decreasing their vibrational frequency, consciousness and growth.

There are three criteria to cultivate Receptivity:

I

Detachment from our limited ego mindset can be a challenging process for all ages due to our various toxic attachments. Some of the most powerful attachments make you mentally and emotionally maligned; which impedes your receptivity and conscious development. People of all ages are becoming addicted to technology; which decreases human bonding and verbal communication. Technology/texting is becoming the predominant form of communication between children, adolescents and adults.

II

Having a strong desire to remember qualities of soul is to have an EMPTY CUP. Every soul has gifts and talents that are pivotal to increasing earth planetary vibrational frequency. When you are motivated by love energy, it allows one to recognize, acknowledge, accept, and creatively cooperate with another individual with different talents and gifts to access their prospective divinity.

III

Humility is the third quality associated with developing receptivity that creates a perpetual learner. Perpetual learning can stimulate remembering your divine soul qualities. Humble people realize that you can learn from everyone. When you are open to learn humbly, you can learn and teach at the same time. Being humble is a 2-way street, one can always be seeking and willing to learn.

> *"You have a choice as to what reality you will experience, for there is more than one door in consciousness. Whichever you choose, your Self will meet you there, either to assist or applaud. Let your choice be the one of your highest ideals, and the vision will be honored."* John Randolph Price, *The Jesus Code*

As a Qi Gong Master, I have had many experiences of learning about student's receptivity. The art of Qi Gong is based on enthusiasm, enjoyment, enhancement, and empowerment. The best Qi Gong Masters realize they're not qualified to judge, that they're only assisting others on their journey and they're not to take responsibility for others on their journey. You only assist based upon the student's receptivity, and you never teach beyond receptiveness.

You can never teach beyond a student's receptivity.

We integrate knowledge based on Receptivity. As you open up to your true self, you awaken to vibrating love, compassion, service and higher frequency. This higher awareness is based in the realness of one COSMIC BREATH, ENERGY and LOVE.

I have always said, "WHEN YOU ARE REAL, YOU CAN DEAL, OTHERWISE CHILL".

And chill means if you don't know, be quiet. A true Master Teacher has no problem with saying "I don't know", while being receptive to knowing. Applied knowledge is empowering and leads to more viable choices.

I envision that if you are reading to this point that you are receptive with an empty cup and an open mind to receive universal truth and wisdom that will raise your vibrational frequency that will stimulate remembering the qualities of your soul and living your Godself.

AFFIRMATION

I am receptive to living my divine true self.

CHAPTER 6

GRATITUDE

Gratitude is a soul quality that stands alone

Gratitude is a soul quality of whole heartedly giving, receiving and sharing from an inner joyfulness. Consciously cultivating an attitude of gratitude increases your mindset which enhances one's health, interpersonal relationships, career path and increases global healing.

The practice of gratitude creates a constant inflow of creative energetic cooperation, in an effortless flow of synchronistic events in your daily life. Even when life throws you a curve ball, it is an opportunity to practice gratefulness and appreciation of one's inner strength. As you practice gratefulness, it becomes a catalyst for developing caring and sharing that increases your vibrational frequency.

> *"As we express our gratitude, we must never forget that the highest appreciation is not to utter words but live by them."*
> John F. Kennedy 1917-1963, 35th President

In other words, there is no need to brag, seeking accolades or recognition. Just have gratitude with joyfulness to appreciate and share in service to humanity.

Practicing gratitude is physically, emotionally, mentally, intellectually and spiritually difficult for the ego oriented individual, because of their selfishness and need to be recognized for giving and sharing. Gratitude is a soul quality that stands alone and is cultivated by having a constant conscious appreciation of all that you own, and all of life's up and down challenges.

I suggest a powerful way of developing gratitude is to take a deep honest look at your physical, mental, emotional, intellectual, and spiritual bodies and scan them to see if you accept them totally without feeling less than or more than any other human being.

After you have done an honest observation of yourself and recognized you may not have accepted all of your different aspects, (and that you are no better than anyone else), it is a golden opportunity to remember and cultivate the soul quality of gratitude.

All individuals (souls) are from the same source with their unique physical, emotional, mental, intellectual and spiritual expressions that is seeking to remember their inner Godself. As one remembers their soul quality of love and gratitude it expands exponentially to other souls to activate soul qualities of love and gratitude. Start practicing with your family, then your community, city, state, country and finally the world. We as individuals, by practicing gratitude, are catalyst for continuous healing and harmonizing the entire planet during this planetary shift.

Are you grateful for your life?

Once you start to understand that you are one with source, you become grateful for everything in your experience. This connection allows you to receive energy to be healthy in your mind, body and spirit.

When you have gratitude, you allow a powerful frequency of love to come into you. You allow it to flow in, let it magnetize and become predominate in your thought.

Now ask yourself a simple question, *are all of your cells magnetized with gratitude and love?*

It is a beneficial practice to give yourself an energetic, visual Love Bath, with your own color of love. (Every human has their color of love, a particular hue that they vibrate to.) Once you bathe yourself in that love, then you can *Smile Love Into your Heart*©. This is referenced in my first book, *Qi Gong Awakens: Always Living in Vibrant Energy* (2013). Whatever color your love is, fill your complete body with love, and with each heartbeat, you will feel love pulsate and vibrate in every cell.

Quantum Physics have proven that thoughts travel. As one focuses on gratitude, it can help each individual and the world frequencies in several ways. It becomes exponential and attracts like-minded people, which is associated with the law of attraction. Once you realize that thoughts have a magnetic force, it is a catalyst to stimulate healing and harmony with oneself, family, communities, country and planet earth.

In closing the chapter of gratitude, **having the attitude of gratitude increases your altitude. You choose.**

AFFIRMATION

I am grateful for all I have and appreciate the
ability to serve.

CHAPTER 7

LIVING YOUR LIFE CHOICE

Living from Clarity and Purpose

To live your life choice is a combination of having clarity and purpose. Purpose leads one to make a definitive decision to follow your life choice. When you consider the power of external distractions of pop culture, religion, peer groups, tribal consciousness plus the current influx of energy on the planet, you find a mentally and emotionally unstable society. People are spending the majority of their life looking outward for stability.

This is compounded by the use of electronic devices at an early age. You now see many little kids have iPads; adolescents addicted to video games and adults also doing this as well. People look to false Gods in the sky, Religions, drugs, materialistic collections, to seek stability and peace. It is easy to look outside of oneself for balance and validation. Letting go of all external validations by looking inside is necessity for harmony and balance.

What is the process of letting go of external attachments?

First, you need to have a stimulus of frustration, irritation, feeling limited, or inner knowing to change from looking from outside to looking inside for stability.

The second thing is relaxation of mental, intellectual, and physical bodies.

The third is to listen and trust your inner voice/feeling and intuition.

The fourth is you must have courage to detach from all external attachments.

The fifth is willpower that you can transcend all opposition.

The sixth is confidence of knowing that all is well. You have the ability to create your happiness and align with your life purpose. Confidence puts you into the frequency of your ancestors, angels and wisdom that all is well.

"Living with vision is walking the line of paradox-

There's loss, there's fullness, love and hate, joy and sadness, exhilaration and fear.

Visionaries know this and are still able to walk the line as they go forward-open to everything that happens and responding accordingly"

Phi Sardella, Organization Development
Consultant

Utilizing the law of intention, involves clarity.

Clarity focuses one's thinking, speaking and action creating a powerful energy of endurance. Often when you decide to live a certain soul quality, (an example is to cultivate kindness, compassion and love), and you are met with life challenges to test your sincerity to live those qualities. Sincerity is a heart frequency that separates the serious individuals from the non-serious individuals from finding and living their life purpose. When you encounter people reflecting sadness, selfishness, and hate, it offers you an optimal opportunity to examine your feelings and judgments. If you feel frustrated, irritated or judgmental, this is confirmation of these unresolved imbalances. On the path to living your choices, you must live in BALANCE. Balance is making an honest choice to cultivate higher frequencies.

If you are an egotistic domineering person, it will be easy to resort to the path of least resistance and low frequency, because you are incapable of expressing love, compassion, and kindness towards others because of the imbalance. Their only concern is being number one and to be pleased. These individuals frequently are articulate with superficial niceness and pretend to care, but their underlying motive is for their own selfish needs.

It is of utmost importance to remember energy always returns to the sender. This is a Universal Law that cannot be manipulated or changed. The statement is:

Whatever you *do*, you *do to yourself*

Ask yourself, "Are you greedy, manipulative, or factual? (Only answering what is asked and withholding the total truth?)"

If you answered Yes to any of these questions, are you willing to be responsible for the consequences of energy returning to you? It usually returns at the least opportune time. And believe me, people frequently blame others for the negative consequences that happens to them. This will affect your daily interaction, family, personal, professional and intimate life. This will give you a powerful lesson where you will have the choice to take total responsibility and turn within using your quality of detachment, confidence, and clarity. You can change your thoughts and actions to be loving, kind, compassionate and grateful. Focusing on these qualities will change your vibration which goes out to the universe and attracts people and places of the same vibrational frequency.

Or you can become reactive not taking any responsibility. The hallmark of adolescence is to blame someone else and play the victim. The concept of blaming is found in all professions, DOCTORS, LAWYERS, TEACHERS, PREACHERS, POLICE OFFICERS, JUDGES, HEALERS, THERAPISTS AND MARKETING PROFESSIONS; anybody can blame others for their own behavior. *Remember all behavior is co-created*. This is where gossip comes in and anyone that participates in gossiping or in toxic energy, is associated with low vibrational frequency, frustration, and inner alienation from their GodSelf.

Once you have a full understanding and acceptance of the law of clarity, living with sincerity enhances remembering qualities of your soul/GodSelf. This choice cultivates energy of GRATITUDE, LOVE, SERVICE, COMPASSION, and KINDNESS.

These frequencies are magnetic which aligns with Universal interconnectedness of One Love, One Breath, and One Energy. In short, remembering and living your soul qualities prepares you to be of greater service to humanity by neutralizing and transforming all isms; racism, sexism, ageism, and homophobia.

The more you honor your path; your individualized energy expands into the flow gives you access to the support of celestial forces full of love and incredible possibilities. To put it another way, you must *individualize to harmonize*. It is hard to harmonize when you are pretending to be someone else.

> *People tend to wear the mask that shows them off in the best possible light-humble, confident, diligent. They say the right things, smile and seem interested in our ideas. They learn to conceal their insecurities and envy. If we take this appearance for reality, we never really know their true feelings, and on occasion we are blind sighted by their sudden resistance, hostility, and manipulative actions. Fortunately, the mask has cracks in it. People continually leak out their true feelings, and unconscious desires in the nonverbal cues they cannot completely control-facial expressions, vocal inflections, tension in the body and nervous gestures.* (Robert Green, p. 72 The Laws of Human Nature)

When you desire to become one with all the energy in your life, you must first become one with yourself. Radiant living can only be generated by the heart, for this is the soul behind all transcendent thought.

When we take the journey of the heart, our connections to the energy around us become clearer. Many people avoid this clarity by living in the intellect. Yet if you desire to become one with the universe and to realize your own incredible potential, the intellect can only get you to the door. It can analyze the wood of the door and the doorknob, but it cannot get you through that door which opens to radiant love. You must have the heart to go through, to accept what you find, to live simply in the beauty of your internal surroundings. Remaining in the realm of analysis makes us far too rigid to flow with the infinite energy of the universe.

Practicing Spiritual/Soulful Qi Gong is a way to allow yourself to cultivate this connection, to purify your heart and to join with the infinite individualized souls of the universe. Think about it, there is one sun with many individualized rays. Each individualized ray shining bright love energy from the Source/God. Wherever God is, I am. Can you look at another life and feel your connection to them? Each of us shining lights is connected to the original source like rays of the sun.

We are all individualized souls on a sacred journey which manifests differently through each of our being. BEAUTY, TRUTH, COURAGE, KINDNESS: these are qualities of our Godself being. Like the air we breathe and the water we drink, we all share truth in its infinite individualized forms from one Source.

AFFIRMATION

I am creating and living my life purpose.

CHAPTER 8

DIVINE WILL

Master Five Qualities

There are two kinds of Will- Divine Will and Ego Will. They are easily distinguished by their purpose and motivation. Divine Will is infused with one love, one energy and one breath and expresses itself through the interconnected to all life. It is in contrast to the egoistic mind which is infused with separatism, selfishness in their personal life and professional life. The egotistic individual is in denial of their Godself, by their delusional belief that there are two separate wills.

"The Will of God is not a God outside of you. It is simply the God that you are and that you have always been, although when you are in a physical incarnation you tend to temporarily forget. Your divine Presence is totally omniscient, omnipresent and omnipotent, and can fulfill all of your desires instantly. You have temporarily forgotten that you are nothing less than an expression of this great I AM, incarnated in a human experience. You came here with an agenda to attain

soul perfection and expand your own divinity to the fullness of your God-Mastery and Wisdom. You are here seeking advanced enlightenment and total spiritual freedom. You are here to become an unlimited God in all planes of existence." Aurelia Louise Jones, *Telos Volume 3–Protocols of the 5th Dimension*

The following qualities of Divine will are critical for navigating through the third dimension. This is dominated by the ego. There is a popular acronym for EGO, Edging God Out. I have created another empowering acronym that is consistent with one's divinity. All souls on the path of spiritually is of the consciousness of EGI

E G I™

Edging God In

(P. L. Hannah, M.D.)

My intention for you reading this book is to focus inwardly towards your inner Godself.

These are the five qualities to live your Divine will:

- Burning Desire
- Detachment
- Courage
- Passion
- Confidence

Burning Desire

Desire to remember your Godself.

Detachment

In the process of detachment, you will encounter strong attachments, living your false self and addictions. These qualities are of the third dimension that vibrates fear, lack and the delusion of separation. Such as in formality of roles, legal, moral, family, peers, race group, religious dogma expectations, personal and professional relationships. These individuals stagnate expressing their Divine will; which causes inner frustration, anxiety, resentment, guilt, anger and boredom. This contributes to the skyrocketing divorce rate due to the emphasis on formality rather than spirituality. There is a huge difference between the formal legal marriage that emphasizes formality, personality (ego), and legality. A spiritual marriage/partnership is focused on soul/spirituality growth while cultivating one's divinity and individuality based upon unconditional love and truth. This relationship might last a few months, a year to a lifetime.

There comes a time when the soul frequencies no longer stimulate growth, inner growth in either one or both partners, which leads to graduation. The graduation is the separation in friendship because it is based on unconditional love, always hoping and expecting for each other the best in terms of optimal growth and soul expression of their individualized gifts and talents. It is like the classical saying: When you love someone set them free. The formalized relationship can co-exist with divine marriage as long as the foundation is the Divine Marriage. However, the reverse is true in our current culture. This is one reason the divorce rate is so high. No other human can marry you. It is a mutual heart/soul matter.

In comparison to the legalized, formalized egotistical marriage there is frequently during the divorce/graduation process; a fight over the materialistic possessions, formality associated with generational habit and expectations of being in the relationship of a lifetime, infidelity (love isn't about ownership) and lingering resentment.

The ancient high vibration frequency Lemurians constantly evaluated the marital relationship to see if there was a match for continued soul development. Unconditional love and soul development was their primary focus compared to legality, formality and material/ money separation.

The vibration on planet earth is stimulating and increasing soul individuality. Individuality is being your true self without any mask, compared to personality wearing masks disconnected from their true self. We must individualize to harmonize. It is extremely challenging for two false personalities to have a healthy joyful, sustaining relationship, because they are both living in a falsehood. They are the great pretenders who live their lives in the sensation of falsehood

Detachment is the process of transcending your attachments with love knowing that the soul will attract people, places, situations that will cultivate your divinity to a frequency of higher joyfulness and freedom. This brings up the third quality of courage.

Courage

Courage is a quality that your voice, your energy is worthy. Your belief, your feelings of divine source energy are equally important to any else in the galaxy.

Passion

Passion is associated with your inner joyful energy fueled by your Godself.

Confidence

Knowing you have source energy to utilize your divine will.

"Self-image must be the awareness of your Holiness, for That is all you are, yet your uniqueness as an Individual comes from many lifetimes of experiences, all of which makes you indispensable in the cosmic process. Do not imitate others or strive to be someone you are not. Value the distinctive contribution you came to make to this world. Know your worth. Be yourself." John Randolph Price

AFFIRMATION

I am divine will living confidently and courageously.

PART 3

KEEP UP

Keeping up is a dynamic process in remembering your soul qualities. It is the phase that separates the *talker* from the *walker*. Many people can talk a persuasive game and can't stay in their lane of manifesting their soul qualities. To continue walking and staying on the path of remembering your soul qualities requires to having an ever-present state of awareness. When one becomes unclear or wavers in their desire to remember their soul, it is easy to shift to the ego, which focuses primarily on the material world, sensation and instinctual human or animal instincts.

Attachment is a frequency that impedes blocks or limits our remembering soul qualities because it is associated with outer energy. Attachment starts from the time of birth, to family, religion, peers, relationships, associates, and employers. Attachment and connection energy have two different vibrational frequencies. As one increases their energetic sensitivity, one can distinguish the difference.

Attachment has a binding energetic strand which leads to limiting one's soul growth and remains in toxic relationships with family, friends, professionals, and employers that do not expand or encourage growth into our unique individualized soul/Godself. The universe is composed of one energy. This connects all things and all people. In being honest with oneself and having the courage to stand in your power and your unique self, embraces our connections. Connected energy allows one in courage and allows one to be free in their individual self A courageous person will be strong enough to let go or detach from people, places or things that limit their being as they access their true self. Our soul essence is that of Creator/God source energy therefore we are energetically Gods and Goddesses with all of the qualities and attributes of God.

Keeping Up is staying connected and associated with like-minded people and having a heart desire, discipline, determination, compassion and unconditional love. Harmony is a quality of being one with self and the universe. As one continues to internalize, there is an increase in the kindness of speech and actions towards others, there is an investment of energy to awake, empower, and expand others to their soul individualized qualities. This deep connection expands to having spiritual vision and allows one to see the beauty in every human being. Expanding the vision of beauty is the cornerstone of being of service to humanity and the planet. This service is associated with faith.

Faith, in essence, is having trust and belief in the Celestial team and the Creator Source God energy, knowing that all is well and that each soul will awaken to their unique individualized Godself. Just imagine that being your Godself; you cannot fail.

CHAPTER 9

LOVE

"Love is the fulfilling of the Law" Romans 13:10

Love is a powerful energetic vibrational frequency that neutralizes, transforms and disintegrates lower energetic frequencies. There are countless definitions of Love, due to individual perceptions, beliefs and uniqueness.

These are some of the dominant features of LOVE in comparison to HATE.

LOVE	HATE
Inclusivity	Exclusivity
Acceptance	Non-acceptance
Non-judgement	Judgement
Unconditional	Conditional
Healing frequency	Harmful frequency
Forgiveness	Grudges
Gratitude	Unappreciation
Humility	Arrogant
Trust	Distrust
Honest	Dishonest
Compassion	Cruelty

Below are the six essential Universal Laws that I will be utilizing in this book.

Please note - I will be teaching other Universal Laws and their applications in my online courses.

Law of One: This law explains the interconnection of energy in humans' animals, rocks, trees, oceans, and Mother Earth. When this law is understood and embraced it generates respect for self, others and mother earth. One consciousness joyfully expands to include all races, religions, political differences and goes to eliminating all the 'isms', like racism, sexism, ageism, socio-economic classism. That is the power of love.

Law of Cause and Effect: This law assures that all energy returns to the sender. In other words, whatever you do, you do to yourself. Look around wherever you are right now, relationships, your job/career, money in the bank, money invested. Do you like what you see? Whatever it is, it is the law of effect fulfilling itself created by you. In other words, if you want amazing relationships, health, and abundance you get all of it depending on the law and its effect. All Spiritual Master Teachers have taught this law to have an ever-present state of consciousness to develop radiant health, youthful energy sustained abundance, and amazing relationships.

Law of Giving: The law of giving is when you give unconditionally, without thank you, recognition, money or favors expected. It is the inner knowing that all is well. That there are unlimited abundance and resources throughout the universe. Giving without expectation, vibrates to the spiritual heart that creates a higher frequency of joyful sharing. Sharing is caring, an enthusiastic expression of love. Whatever you desire give it away. If you give unconditional love you receive that. When you tithe unconditionally based upon spiritual teaching you receive it back 10-fold What are you giving, sharing or caring unconditionally? Be radically honest with yourself in answering this question.

Balance

Giving unconditionally and receiving unconditionally with gratitude

When there is an imbalance in giving and receiving it is associated with multiple layers of fear, lack, greed and rejection.

When someone has problems receiving, there is a feeling of not being worthy, and a lack of appreciation.
Divine balancing is joyfully giving and receiving with gratitude which is also a component of unconditional love.

Law of Harmony: The law of harmony is associated with the balance of your soul energy. This is aligned with the Universal Energy. A major lesson of one's soul reincarnation to the Earth plane is to remember oneness with source energy. During the process of learning on the earth plane one has to be totally responsible for aligning all of your mental, emotional spiritual bodies without blaming any situation or any individuals for what happens to us. We create our own life based upon thought process, in doing this we must maintain balance. Being in balance is a pillar for creating and maintaining radiant health, relationships and professional career. When one is responsible and balanced it leads to one's divine alignment with soul purpose. Alignment is associated with synchrony, this can be noticed or felt because of the effortless flow of life.

"Synchronicity is always on the move and is dynamic, depending on how often you listen to intuitive potentials that are given to you. There will always be people for you to meet. There are always good things available. Synchronicity is a benevolent energy that is designed to help you. Are you taking advantage of this?" Kryon, *The New Human*

Law of Attraction: The law of attraction is a universal energetic magnetic scientific law. Your thoughts create a vibrational frequency which matches the universal energy that manifests on the physical plane.

"The first and most important thing to understand and to accept without question is the fundamental law of life thought precedes every action from the most minor to the most profoundly important. It's the "way you think" which determines the life you will have, it can make you enormously successful or dismal failure, it can give you love and happiness or a life of loneliness and misery.

The second most important thing to understand and to accept without question is that "it is you" and you alone who decides the "way you think." The only thing which is immediately available to you, over which you have total and exclusive control, and which is totally private to you is the way you think. The way you think is the most powerful influence in your life and is, in effect you." Brian Kahlefeldt, *Ninety Minutes to Success*

It is important to have clarity and an ever-present state of consciousness before you speak your thoughts. Are you aware of your current thoughts if not take a sincere honest and detached inner observation of your feelings, thoughts and beliefs?

Observe are you happy with yourself. Are you creating joyful, happy experiences with family friends' coworkers? Are you financially secure or overwhelmed with credit card debt? Are you contributing to global healing and harmony or stuck in the tribal consciousness of separatism, hate and disharmony? Remember whatever your answer you co created it. You are responsible for your health, possession, financial status and experiences around you. YOU ARE THE CREATOR OF YOUR LIFE. You can only blame yourself.

"Love is the fulfilling of the Law" Romans 13:10

Law of Relativity: This law is a universal energetic scientific tool that can be utilized to develop and expand one's divinity. There are approximately 8 billion people on planet earth, each person has their own unique thumb print and soul lessons throughout this incarnation. As we go through life there will be ups and downs on your path and depending on your degree of your attachment to people places and things. Sometimes your pain is more penetrating, and the intensity is associated with 3 powerful qualities:

- comparing
- judgment
- lack of acceptance

This is when the law of relativity comes into play. If you continue to go outward, by using social media, blindly following religion or looking for external validation, then it can lead to depression, anger, and a total imbalance in one's emotion and thinking.

While utilizing the essence of the law of relativity in your awareness; ask yourself: Have you accepted your true self or your false self-supported and accepted by society?

In my book *Qi Gong Awakens*, on page 40, I share about "Radiant Acceptance."

> *"The more you accept yourself and the world in which you live, the higher your energy frequency will rise. As your frequency rises, you will welcome more truth into your life. By digesting this truth and radiating it out into the world, you will be able to radiate your light in the world. This radiance is unlimited by judgment."*

Judgment and comparison are the function of the ego that are a blockage to living your Godself. The sincere truth seeker utilizes the law of relativity when analyzing life experiences as beneficial or stagnating. Experiences are deemed good or bad depending on one's perception.

Another aspect of dealing with the law of relativity is absolute truth. The truth is unchangeable, and every soul is endowed with guidance of the absolute truth.

However, all souls have different level of awareness and truth. One example:

A person swimming in a pond cannot measure a person in the sea and a person in the sea cannot measure the person in the ocean.

> *"The criteria for recognizing, measuring and knowing the truth is the amount of truth you have in yourself."*
> Dr. David M. Berry

Confusion and conflict can emerge from that statement. There is no argument of truth, it is. The person who has the highest level of truth is usually quiet with compassion. There is no need to argue with someone else who has lesser truth.

Love can be understood by using the laws of relativity. There are many kinds of love; puppy love, high school love, adult love, father love, mother love, agape love, LGBTQ love, family love, brother and sister love.

All these types of love are associated with inclusivity, unconditional acceptance, courage, and honesty. They are expressions of the one love, one energy and one breath.

> *"You can always choose another way if you realize that the direction you choose leads away from the light, because the path that doesn't lead to the heart is illusion"* Lars Muhly, *The Law of Light*

AFFIRMATION

I am Love frequency uniting energetic oneness.

CHAPTER 10

COURAGE

"The cultivation of your spirit creates a ripple effect throughout the universe. Do not underestimate the power of your gift. Countless souls will be impacted by what you have to offer."
James Weeks, *Meditations Across the King's River*

Divine Courage is an energetic quality which motivates one to joyfully live or die for their soul purpose/cause. Courage gives one freedom to express their individuality/truth regardless of how many people are against their beliefs, causes, feelings, and purpose. Courage also has the ability to detach from your family generational beliefs and consciousness.

"A man who does not have something for which he is willing to die for is not fit to live." Dr. Martin Luther King

When I heard, felt and agreed with Dr. King's courageous and stimulating speech, it was a pivotal point in my life. In essence everyone's life will be enriched when they live with courage and freedom to live or die.

Do you have the **courage** to live your joyful Godself?

Living with courage and freedom, cultivates a mindset of living in the nowness. There is NO yesterday or tomorrow, only NOW. One's quality of life is based upon their courageous nowness.

Someone that exemplifies this courageous principle is President Nelson Mandela, who refused to change his beliefs and faced life in prison. He maintained his integrity and principles and became stronger during his incarceration and eventually became the President of South Africa. He demonstrated the Godself values of courage, soul purpose and alignment.

We have some great examples of men and women who demonstrated great courage to uphold their values. Dr. Martin Luther King and President Mandela were willing to give up everything to live and express their principles. Doy Gorton (a Caucasian) who lived in the deep south during the racist white supremacist movement, joined the civil rights movement and was killed while photographing these marches. Mahatma Ghandi employed nonviolent resistance to gain independence for India from British rule was assassinated for his beliefs. Pedro Albuizu Campos was a powerful orator who left his teaching position in the US and went to Puerto Rico to rally his people towards independence and was imprisoned and exposed to radiation and died. Harriet Tubman, a powerful black woman, who exemplified courage and freedom to free many Black slaves to Canada in the underground railroad. And let's not forget Jesus the Christ also exemplified courage based on unconditional love.

If you look at the above examples you will see that there is a common thread among them that they were living their passion aligned with their soul purpose and principles. These courageous individuals were willing to take on the ultimate test of death, incarceration, detachment and being outcast from their tribal /family consciousness, racial, political and financial position.

> *"Free yourself from any mental, emotional, physical or societal prisons in which you have boxed yourself. Free yourself from creating your next moment based on opinions of the past. Create your next moment on an in-the-beginning consciousness."* Michael Bernard Beckwith, *Transcendence Expanded*

These examples exemplify alignment with soul purpose, principle motivated by the inclusivity of love which neutralizes exclusivity, separation, hatred, racism, and ignorance.

In conclusion, remember courage is needed for living your life purpose and remembering your soul qualities and living your Godself.

> *"Keep continuity of consciousness with the communication you are receiving on a continuous basis, every second. Live with a poised mind, allowing the Self to come through all time, as you learn to integrate the higher mind with the mental mind and the body."* Barbara Marx Hubbard, *52 Codes for Conscious Self Evolution*

AFFIRMATION

I am endowed with divine courage, living day by
day my joyful Godself way.

CHAPTER 11

COMPASSION

**Compassion is a heart frequency vibration, with a
foundation in love and respect**

Compassion's Heart frequency vibration includes the feeling of love that goes to the core of your Godself. This love is inspiring and accepting. There is no manipulation or domination. It is associated with joyful acceptance, individuality and giving unconditionally from the heart.

Love and respect are incorporated with the Law of Cooperation. I have found as a Healer Psychiatrist, and Master martial artist, that aligning your mental, emotional, physical, intellectual and spiritual bodies develops your internal coordination. This alignment offers great awareness, sensitivity and feeling developing your divine self. An increase in your vitality and radiance results when you align your mental, emotional, spiritual, physical and intellectual bodies. When you align all of them with self-love and respect, that energetic frequency attracts you to another similar frequency.

"Out of love and respect for ourselves and others, we don't put our tensions on anybody else. Instead we learn about surrender. We think a lot about it and try to understand it, because of our understanding of surrender a state of openness emerges. Our hearts and minds become open and, in that openness, we begin to perceive the thread that unites one person and another in divine dance of creation." Swami Chetanananda, *Open Heart, Open Mind*

Sometimes people are under the delusion that there are two selves. The Ego self has to be against something or someone due to its limited nature. In the Godself, there is no need to dominate because there is one energy, one breath, one love. There is no need for win or lose, right or wrong. Abundance is available in the Godself.

To experience and connect to your Godself, you must surrender with the courage to let go. We want to free the Ego self which has the desire to win, to be right, dominate. Egotistical minded individuals function primarily in the third dimension.

David McArthur & Bruce McArthur shared their insights on dimensions that can help us. Let's look at these classifications of Dimensions:

Dimension	Attribute
5th	Divine purpose is accomplished
Higher 4th	Accessed through heart. Transformation efficiency-powerful Brings change to 3rd

Dimension	Attribute
Middle 4th	Inner change. Religion /ritual. Processing. Moderate energy Weak effect on 3rd
Lower 4th	Social responsibility. Slow change
3rd	Physical focus/self-focus

Developing divine compassion involves cultivating your heart frequency to a higher level at the 5th dimension and this higher frequency is associated with the Law of Light.

As one develops more divine light and the courage to see reality as it is with clear vision, you develop a victorious mentality. While being victorious, you navigate life challenges regardless how toxic it might be. Experiences such as sudden ill health, poor finances, unsatisfactory professional relationships, intimate relationships, or living a life of desperation are viewed as a great opportunity to learn and transcend to a higher expansive love energy frequency.

When you have the intention of developing self-compassion, do you accept your body and all its configurations, colors, or shapes? Do you compare yourself egotistically with others? When you see people less fortunate, in emotional pain or having difficulty graduating from life experiences, do you empathize or sympathize?

When you get in the habit of sympathy, you are perpetuating a judgmental, separatist belief which is also a reflection of you. If you answered yes to any of these questions you have clouded your ability to feel your divine compassion.

This also develops empathy rather than sympathy. Empathy is associated with compassion and seek to empower the person in need. Your inherent divinity is respectful and responsible and views life challenges as a blessing because it allows one to graduate from limiting, toxic situations. The good news is that once you graduate you don't have to repeat it.

As you go forward and graduate from these life experiences with love and respect and a victorious mentality it increases your compassion power. That capacity is unified in the law of oneness, law of cooperation, law of light, forgiveness and most of all unconditional love. The unconditional love continues to fuel kindness and compassion.

One beneficial way of remembering and developing your divine compassion qualities is to begin with a quality that you have difficulty in accepting. Focus on that thought with love in your heart especially when you get up the morning and at bedtime. Smile that thought into your heart. If you do this for 21 days your subconscious mind will be impregnated with your new compassionate quality. You feel, act and think and believe as if already exists. Congratulation in advance on the completion of your 21 days and joyfully expanding that vibration throughout the planet.

AFFIRMATION

I am compassionate with myself and others.

CHAPTER 12

BEAUTY

Beauty is in the Heart of the Beholder

B eauty is an infinite divine quality of the soul. To fully appreciate beauty, one must observe from the divine eyes rather than the physical eyes. I find that natural beauty is displayed by the cyclical four seasons.

Nature is a master designer of coordinating colors and designs. The Springtime represents new life that emerges from the frigid winter. Spring has a fresh and inspiring energy which is reflected in the budding flowers and greenery of the shrubs. When I walk in the woods, I smell the sweet fragrance of the flowers and the green buds have a powerful effect of stimulating relaxation and clarity of my mind; which enhances my sensitivity and vibrational frequency. One with nature, I breath in oxygen and exhale carbon dioxide and the trees inhale carbon dioxide and exhale oxygen. It is a beautiful example of the law of reciprocation.

As Spring transcends to Summer, there is a continuation of the beautiful flowers, birds singing, the smell of lilacs and roses. You can sense the grass growing, the fragrance of flowers, budding trees, and the bees pollinating the flowers.

The colors express their own frequency and vibration. The colors affect people whether they are aware of it or not. Some people are sensitive to the colors and their frequency. This is brilliantly utilized by flower essence medicine. When I was in Brazil, I could feel the different temperature and flowers, based on the color of the flower it emitted different levels of coolness and energy.

Nature continues as a Master Gardener of design, manifesting in the variety of color of leaves on the trees. Red, yellow, brown, orange is highlighted and signal the change of Summer to Fall creating a beautiful spectrum of colors. These colors have a beautiful uplifting effect, because of the harmonious display. The change of the smell from grass to wood effects the frequency felt in the Fall. Continuing to the Winter is a smooth transition, the process of recycling is expressed by the leaves become fertilizer and mulch, creating energy to the plants and flowers in the Spring. Energy becomes dormant in the trees during the Winter.

There are museums all around the world that house beautiful paintings, sculptures and drawings. The Art's beauty stimulates attendee's inner divinity and expands their vibrational frequency to the heart. Love reflects the beauty and love is Inclusive-It is the law of oneness.

I enjoy listening to opera because of its beauty. The octave energetic frequency stimulates my heart and throat chakra. It has multiple benefits; refines my clairsentience, distinguishing the difference when people are speaking/singing from their mouth, heart or throat.

I am a conduit for transmitting unconditional love and universal truth. The heart chakra represents unconditional love and the throat chakra speaking compassionate truth. You can get the same experience listening to poetry, artistic dancing, ballet, musicals or music concerts. All of these expressions raise the vibration throughout the planet.

> "In everything that is living even in things we consider to be inanimate there is a hidden beauty which one might call the archetypal perfection. That beauty which is in the heart of things will shine forth through us in every act if there is no self, but only the energy of love to shape our action." N. Sri Ram, Thoughts for Aspirants

Remembering the quality of beauty in your soul requires cultivating the following laws:

The Law of One

The law of one emphasizes that everyone and everybody is energetically interconnected.
When one is viewing beauty, it is activating a heart frequency, planetary and others vibrational frequency.

The Law of Intention

The law of intention requires one having clarity of your desire. Clarity increases focus, when your intention is planted in the subconscious mind it increases the manifestation of this, therefore it focuses ability to see beauty in yourself and others

The Law of Action

The law of action is associated with begetting in other words you get what you give. Your vibration matches what you give out. It also is noted in physics. 'Sir Isaac Newton. "Every action has an equal reaction." Therefore it is important to have this.

The Law of Harmony

The law of harmony is living from the alignment of emotional, mental, physical bodies which is the harmony of your authentic/Godself. When you align with yourself the harmonic frequency goes out and magnetizes other people of the same frequency.

The Law of Unity

The law of unity, given that all energy is connected, and in animation this law is crucial for expanding the heart energy creating purification and unification.

Integration of the above laws is the cornerstone of remembering your soul's beauty, because you will see the beauty of yourself. It connects and expands divine frequency of the planet and others from the heart.

As we create beauty we look around for beauty in other people, surround yourself with beautiful flowers, sculptures and paintings. Beauty is a high frequency vibration as you open your heart up to unconditional love. Beauty is a perpetual giver of love energy and inspiration, asking for no validation because it a standalone soul quality. This internal radiant beauty, vibrates from inside out and doesn't need any facial creams to shine out

How do we embody beauty?

Radiant beauty comes when we begin to express inner harmony through our eyes, our smile, our movements, and our touch. It cannot be purchased or achieved. It can only be accepted and allowed. Like all spiritual qualities, radiant beauty is a gift. One that we must prepare ourselves to receive. Both a feeling and a visual truth, radiant beauty is something that is both known deep inside and is recognized by receptive eyes and a heart of love.

Our natural beauty flows from our personal uniqueness, harmony, and joy. When we accept our uniqueness, commit to our harmony, and claim our joy, then we automatically become more radiant. A special light takes root in our inner core and beauty shines out from there. When we relax into this beauty, remembering that it is an expression of who we were meant to be, then the world around us also becomes more enchanting.

Nobody on earth has the same divine appearance as us. No one has our exact same energy or thumb print. Yet we are linked to everyone and everything. We are simultaneously one-of-a-kind and perfectly connected.

When our connection to our Godself is bright and clear, this connection shines from every pore of our most beautiful being. We become a unique and joyful expression of an infinitely larger harmony. The way we smile, how we walk, the words that leave our lips; these all become personal manifestations of the universal energy that moves through us.

Radiant beauty communicates this natural energy to everyone who is ready to receive the message. This message is open to everyone, regardless of skin color, of weight, and of personality type. We all carry with us the potential for incredible joy and for radiant life.

Realizing this potential means embracing the energy of growth, change, and expansion. It means declaring to the world:

I know who I am, I know why I am here, and I know that I am a part of a great cosmic adventure.

On this adventure there is little time for thoughts or actions that do not serve the Divine.

Nobody is Qualified to Judge

Access to the soul quality of beauty allows you to let go of every thought and action which is not a part of your most radiant self. It allows you to move beyond judgment and deception by moving towards acceptance, radiant beauty and truth.

When we judge one another, we are disconnected from the reality of our own radiance and the beauty of those around us. We momentarily lose the vibrant awareness of who we really are. In the whirlwind of judging, we lose sight of the radiance within both ourselves and the people we are attempting to judge.

Surviving each new day of life demands that we observe our surroundings, that we make real decisions based on these observations, and that we pay special attention to any extraordinary events or energies that we encounter. Yet all of this can be done with a heart of appreciation and discernment, rather than judgment and critique. Only then can we keep sight of our own incredible energy, as well as the greater beauty to which we are connected.

Once we realize that nobody is qualified to judge, then we can keep the mental awareness and emotional flexibility required to see the immense opportunity that is always present in our lives. Every breath we take represents this opportunity, the promotion of a greater now, of a more complete self, of more loving relationships, or of a more harmonious world. Radiant beauty serves as a testament to all of these possibilities. All of these possibilities start becoming realities when we align our consciousness with our breath. Breathing with consciousness, and remembering who we are, is an essential dimension of claiming our radiant beauty.

> *"Beauty needs no justification. If one creates something of real beauty it is a part of what should exist, no part of any personal achievement. Everything really beautiful in life can be found and is to be found within one's self."* N. Sri Ram, *Thoughts for Aspirants*

AFFIRMATION

I am beautiful and recognize beauty in all forms of life.

CHAPTER 13

SERVICE

Divine Unconditional Love

Service is a divine act which embodies unconditional love, truth and purpose. To serve someone is to awaken them to their inner divinity, where they are able to help themselves. The most effective way to awaken an individual's inner divinity is by personally vibrating unconditional love, truth and purpose.

This creates the vibrational frequency that can spread throughout the universe. Example: 1 helps 10, 10 helps 100, 100 helps 10,000, to 100,000, to 1,000,000 as it spreads exponentially throughout the galaxy because of the law of oneness.

Love energy is distinguished between judgment vs. discernment, accepting vs. tolerating, inclusiveness vs. exclusiveness. Which is from the Source/God energy that is non-judgmental accepting and inclusive vs trying to control and manipulate people.

At 12 years old, I realized intuitively the propaganda, manipulation and trying to control people based on the erroneous pictorial presentation of the bible. The falsehood that was promoted was when you commit a sin you burn in hell forever which is inconsistent with unconditional love and forgiveness. In the church where I grew up, the bible was represented by a White Jesus or all white men. I witnessed no racial or gender inclusivity, already an imbalance which reflected the underlying fear and insecurity. When I saw the angels; there were predominately white males and few females. No Black, Brown, Yellow or Red angels; which disqualifies someone from servicing people to them awaken to their own divinity. It excludes unconditional love or the absolute truth.

So therefore, it is impossible to offer service to someone when the whole foundation is based on conditionality. That same predominately white male yang energy continues to perpetuate a continued imbalance and the falsehood. This old paradigm is being transformed because we are now living on the plane of manifestation that is about unity, balance, joy, and love.

People are seeking for their inner divinity and will no longer be suppressed, controlled or dominated. People are rising with courage. Females are rightfully seeking balance and the freedom to express their own individuality. *Everyone must balance their male and female energy.* This creates a more harmonious law of cooperation. People are no longer willing to be controlled by the white male yang energy that is about domination and manipulation.

The new influx of 5th dimension energy is awakening the inner divinity of people of all races and it is forcing people to balance the feminine energy of all humans. Due to the reincarnation of light workers being born right now, each one has their own unique gift that is geared toward service to humanity.

Musicians from all types of music including hip hop, classical, blues, or reggae are expressing their gifts and divinity to stimulate people to wake up to their own <u>divinity</u>. From cab drivers, janitors, nannies, teachers, gardeners, doctors, they are all seeking their divinity. Remember everyone that you encounter is a reflective mirror of you. Therefore, clarifying, confirming, and inspiring you to be more your authentic Godself.

The predominance of yang energy is finite. No sums of money, no mass incarceration or killing will be able to stop the transformation all over the galaxies, because of the strong desire and courage that is awakening their inner divinity and soul quality.

In this plane of manifestation all secrets will be exposed; it is part of the purification process. Even Mother Earth is waking up as expressed by climate change, volcanic eruptions, tsunamis, by reacting to the greed and ignorant abuse. The time is changing for there to be a mass influx of love energy to raise the vibrational frequency. This purification will bring harmonization. There is a mass waking up and remembering by people seeking their way back to their divine home. Some would call it heaven, but it really is within each and every one of us.

With the advanced technology, and the influx of light workers being born with their unique talents and gifts, they are expediting communication vibrational frequency and awakening the individual divinity. That divinity is creating a global vibrational frequency uniting on one love, one breath one energy.

REMEMBERING QUALITIES OF YOUR SOUL

You are creating a frequency of like attracts like.

I am joyful to see the influx of light workers of all races, all walks of life, who are attracted to infinite level of love, beauty and abundance. Their inner divinity vibrates at a high level where there is unlimited abundance.

In conclusion, when you desire to serve it is imperative to examine your thoughts and beliefs that have been perpetuated for thousands of years by Roman Empire, Greeks, who have been impregnated in your subconscious mind of the falsehoods and white male dominance.

This is not limited to white people, any race or color (Chinese, Hispanic, or African, Arabs). We all have been bought into the game of white male dominance (or male dominance) and white privilege from the bible to experience this social status. Even education has accepted the same beliefs of dominance. There has been benefit from these false beliefs, and they will have to take a close look at the subconscious cellular beliefs, feelings and behavior as they have to be neutralized in order to be of true service. When everyone expresses their divine light and love we will move from this fear of lack of third dimension mindset, to a consciousness of abundance and inclusivity in the 5th dimension.

"I AM obedient to God within me now.

I AM the presence of God

Knowing all things,

Thinking all things,

Being all things,

That are of service

To the Light."

Step by Step Edited by Peter Mt. Shasta

AFFIRMATION

I am a divine servant joyfully utilizing my gifts to
awaken and help others.

CHAPTER 14

FAITH

If you Believe it, you can Receive It

This is how I define FAITH:

FAITH – FOLLOWING ANGELS IN TO HEAVEN ™

Let's look at each word for the deeper meaning.

FOLLOWING is the act of detaching from the ego mind and allowing the Divine mind, which is infinite. I discuss Allowing in my first book, *Qi Gong Awakens: Always Living in Vibrant Energy.* Allowing is believing in the invisible force that is beyond the five senses in this physical domain known as source energy or God... There is a knowing that is associated with trust, belief, purpose and divine energy.

"For we live by faith, not by sight" 2 Corinthians, 5:7

ANGELS are an invisible celestial energy resource available for our asking. There are a number of angels and their hierarchy, and they will not interfere with your soul path or daily decision unless you ask. You must ask with sincerity from your heart for what you need. There are no limitations to your questions.

I've encountered patients and students who are dominated by the ego mind. When you are dominated by the ego mind it is associated with limitations and depression and the belief that *no invisible or physical can help them.* There is an internal emotional pain that leads to drug and substance abuse, eating disorders, starving for attention which leads to easy manipulation and victimization. Dominated by a sense of lack their thoughts create that vibrational frequency which becomes a perpetual cycle.

> *"Igbagbo is the Yoruba word for faith. Igbagbo requires you to see with inner eyes and hear with inner ears. No great vision comes to fruition without faith."* James Weeks, *Meditations across the King's River*

INTO is a process of going deeper in your divinity. There are multiple spiritual laws that utilize going into the energy of oneness. The law of oneness transcends duality, it is always vibrating at a frequency of wholeness.

Energy of cooperation is the giving and receiving that harmoniously benefits the individual who is operating from their divine heart. That is dealing from divine mind to divine mind. When you encounter people that trigger toxic emotions, the energy of cooperation helps you realize that the person is mirroring your emotional pain. When you view this mirroring of the individual with gratitude it will enhance the remembering qualities of the soul and expand your divine vibrational frequency.

HEAVEN is a process of receiving the harvest of one's faith. which is associated with the law of abundance, detachment and harmony:

- Abundance means there is no limit of supply. All limitations are mentally imposed by the individual. Holding a clear thought infused with heart desire and patience, brings abundance.

- Harmony is a process of being aligned with your mental emotional and spiritual bodies creating a balanced frequency which matches the harmonious frequency of the universe. This is a synchronistic process where you find life moving in a joyful effortless manner.

- Detachment is the process of letting go of the outcome. There is trust in the universal intelligence process as to when, where, and the time a goal is manifested. To connect with your Godself you must be joyfully patient.

AFFIRMATION

I am faithful in the divine process of manifesting all
my goals.

PART 4

ENERGETIC TECHNIQUES

I am Fueling my Godself

As you wake up and remember, living one's soul qualities requires tremendous amounts of energy to sustain optimal health. Energy is required to create and maintain life. Part V will talk about techniques to develop and expand one's radiant physical health and awakening to your true eternal Godself.

The body is the temple of the soul and is to be honored and protected from energy of mental, emotional, environmental and fast food destruction. Breathing in Qi/Prana life force sustains the physical world. Our physical life begins with inhalation and transition in the spiritual realm with the final exhalation. There are many effective techniques of breathing, that are utilized for relaxation, concentration, meditation, mantras and imagination. Daily practice of being quiet, meditation, chanting, praying and inner listening will enhance your ability to detach from limiting thoughts, people and connecting to universal truth and unconditional love.

Sound vibration is primal in creating the physical world. Being relaxed praying, chanting (static and shaking) can activate our true selves and increase sensitivity to hear, feel, see and communicate with invisible spiritual energy communicating with ancestors, angel and guides. Intuition is utilized to lead one to higher vibrational frequency and dimensions as well as protecting one from dangerous people, places and situations.

Movement on a daily basis is needed to maintain radiant health. It keeps us strong and vibrant and decreases our chances of acquiring dis-ease processes. Medical literature on maintaining health and preventing dis-ease is to practice 150 mins/week, it is preferred to 30 mins times 5 days a week. There are many different types of exercise you can do to get your 150 mins; walking, running, swimming, cycling, yoga, dancing, resistant and weight training, Tai Chi Chuan, Martial Arts (internal and external), boxing, and tennis.

The body is 70% water therefore drinking alkaline, spring water or reverse osmosis is essential in maintaining optimal energy for radiant health. Proper hydration is essential for the metabolism, detoxification, circulation of transporting nutrient to the cells and neurological impulse throughout the brain and body. To fully hydrate to elevate to a higher frequency one method to measure proper hydration is to measure your waist in inches and multiply x2 in ounces. An example, if your waist in 30 inches it means that 60 oz. is needed for proper hydration.

Whether one chooses to be breatharian, vegan, vegetarian or carnivorous it is a personal choice. There are centurions who are vegan, vegetarians and carnivores. Having an attitude of love and gratitude, chewing slowly and being quiet can affect the optimal nutrients extracted for your body use. Follow your intuition to guide you to the proper nutrition to maintain optimal functions. One must be careful and distinguish eating habits from your higher intuition from your lower ego. Lower ego eating habits have toxic intake of sugar, salt and saturated fats; decreasing your vital energy and increases obesity, hypertension, diabetes, inflammatory disease and cancer. This style of eating is showing lack of love for themselves and disrespecting the body temple. When you love you take care, the question is:

Do you love, care or honor your temple?

You be the judge and be responsible for all the consequences of your choices.

Eating ample fruits and vegetables of different colors increases getting nutrients, vitamins, minerals, and proteins. Higher quantity of antioxidants from plants decreases free radical disease causing affects. When there are more free radicals than anti-oxidants it is the internal environment for creating a disease process. Plant based proteins are easier to digest and don't increase cholesterol and blood sugar spikes.

Ideally through eating and juicing vegetables, fruits and nuts one can get proper nutrition. Due to the depleted minerals in the soil it is necessary to supplement to get optimal nutrition. Walking in the sun while sweating helps convert Vitamin D3 and vitality to the body. I recommend being in the sun early in the morning and late afternoon to avoid toxic ultraviolet rays, it can be associated with developing skin cancer. Other supplementation for optimal health, are Vitamins A, C, E, CQ10, selenium, L-Carnitine, Glutathione, Iodine, B complex, Magnesium. Plant based and fermented are suggested. This is only a partial list of basic supplements.

There are good fats needed for optimal fuel development; avocado, walnuts, flax, coconut, extra virgin olive oil, omega 3 oil, and MCT oil. In addition, follow your intuition and consider getting a holistic, spiritual, nutritional specialist to create your individualized treatment plan.

Fasting and calorie reduction are proven to be associated anti-aging detoxification and increasing energy. Starting with 16 hours for three, seven, fourteen days.

CHAPTER 15

BREATH

Let every breath activate your Godself

B reathing generates essential energy for creating and maintaining human life. The energy that separates life from death, or should I say human being from spiritual being on the material plane, is breath. Physically, breath is composed of the 2 components; inhaling and exhaling.

Inhaling begins at birth which activates brain waves, heartbeat and lung functions. The final exhale occurs at physical death when the brainwave, heartbeat and lungs cease functioning.

When a human baby is born and the umbilical cord is surgically cut, by the Midwife, Doula, Nurse, or Physician, the baby begins to naturally breathe from their belly (Dan Tien). Breathing from the Dan Tien is associated with having more vital energy, relaxation, creativity, well-being and endurance. The Dan Tien is the focus of attention for meditation, relaxation, expanding love frequency, resolving severe anxiety, and anger.

As a Healer, Physician, Soulful/Spiritual Qi Gong Master and Internal Martial Artist, I have had ample opportunity to observe students, patients and professionals be unaware of how to do natural breathing. When they cultivate breath from the Dan Tien, they develop more energy, endurance, relaxation and vitality. According to Dr. Jim Deaver, when you slow down your breathing it slows the heart rate. He found that slower breath brings about a general relaxation of all internal body functions which in turn lowers your blood pressure.

I find that cultivating breath is the cornerstone for having radiant health. This is well known to professional athletes, martial artists, Masters of Qi Gong and Tai Chi Chuan, Yoga Gurus, and Reiki healers. As you become more efficient in breathing, your relaxation, sensitivity and ability to receive and transmit universal high vibrational frequency energy expands exponentially. This expansive energy is associated with a clear reflective mirror and a divine catalyst therefore, making one a better teacher/healer/professional.

There are many types of meditations that require various styles of breathing, it enhances performers, singing opera, reciting mantras, they all utilize natural breath.

The process of developing conscious breath must start with a desire and an intent to connect with your divine Godself.

You must be able to relax your whole body. What I learned in martial arts was that I had to stand, relax my total body, place my tongue on roof of my mouth, and relax my shoulders while my spine is straight. At the same time, you relax your chest, arms and fingers. Then you observe your breath naturally so that when you inhale your stomach inflates and when you exhale your stomach deflates.

In this way, the relaxation process is going from your head to your feet. If you feel there is tension, you can feel it, and then smile and release. In my first book, *Qi Gong Awakens* (P. L. Hannah), I share my technique of *smiling love into your heart*. It is a very powerful technique for relaxing your mental, emotional and physical bodies. This Heart aligned love frequency enhances performance artists, teachers, healers, to transmit universal energy to others.

Whether you are sitting or standing the same applies.

Proper breathing Technique:

- If you are sitting down in a chair with your spine straight,
- Chin slightly down,
- Eyes closed,
- Tongue at the top of the mouth,
- Relaxed facial muscles,
- Neck and shoulders down,
- Sink and relax your chest,
- Hands in one of 3 positions:
    1. Hold both hands towards your Dan Tien or
    2. Cupped over knees keeping energy contained within you or
    3. Palms turned up to the sky to receive universal love energy,
- Hips relaxed, feet on the floor shoulder width apart.
- You gently focus your mind on your Dan Tien no force,

- Inhale and Exhale, your stomach is inflating while you inhale, your stomach is deflating while you exhale.

Whether you are sitting or standing the same applies.

As a healer and martial artist, I am sensitive to hear the flow of one's breath. Whether my student or patient are breathing through their nose, mouth or chest it will limit their sensitivity, energy flow and endurance. With my patients and students, I can determine whether they are

Different breathing awareness:

- Breathing through nose congested breathing which may be associated with allergies, due to eating foods that you are allergic to. (Eg. Cheese, wheat, peanuts, shellfish, garlic and eggs).
- Mouth breathing can be associated with asthma, upper respiratory infection, emphysema, or bad habits.
- Chest breathing may be associated with fear, anxiety, depression, becoming a master of over accommodating instead of having the courage of being your true self.

Compare your breathing to a baby who is breathing naturally from the Dan Tien bringing in universal energy in the flow.

Ancient practices taught proper breathing for centuries. Yoga, Qi Gong and Reiki have one commonality of bringing more love-light energy into the body. Light energy with Yoga is alignment of your body and spirit through breathing, stretching, and using asanas relaxation and light. In Reiki, one becomes a channel of receiving and transmitting light. The Soulful Spiritual Qi Gong that I practice brings in universal light primarily through the heart chakra.

> *"When mankind perceives reality though an open, evolved heart chakra, mortal man experiences reality by "feeling the energy states of that reality."* Akhenaton, Discussions of Spiritual Attunement & Soul Evolution Vol. II

I will be teaching how to develop natural breathing in my 2 online courses, Breath Cultivation for Developing Soulful Qualities and Awakening Purifying and Aligning the Primary Seven Chakras.

Breathing from the Dan Tien is important for developing and maintaining energy as we go through life remembering qualities of the soul. Prana is a vital force that pervades the Cosmos and this energy goes throughout the universe. When we breath in the subtle energy, mastering meditation we can control the amount of prana that flows into the body.

Just imagine when you are breathing you are bringing in more prana from the universe.

> *"Many ancient cultures, such as the Incas, Egyptians and Tibetans, believed in and taught breathing exercises for healing purposes and to raise consciousness. Mystics and gurus believed that practicing pranayama led to the experiencing of the true self and the universe. The Christ talked about the sacredness of breath in the Dead Sea Scrolls: "We revere the holy breath which is beyond all creation. For behold, the eternal, highest realm of light, where the infinite star's*

reign, is the realm of air, which we inhale and exhale. And in the moments between inhalation and exhalation, all the mysteries of the eternal garden are hidden". The Buddha used conscious breathing to achieve enlightenment and the Native Americans Indians and Sufis include breathing practices in their initiating rites. The Indian Guru Maharishi Mahesh Yogi who developed Transcendental Meditation technique said: "Through control of the breath we achieve control over the mind, and by controlling the mind we return to the original state of Eden." Pauline Wills, *Yoga of Light*

Practicing turtle breathing in Qi Gong is utilized for developing radiant health and longevity. Turtle breathing creates a deeper sense of relaxation and inner calmness. This reduces toxic stress the major cause of chronic, debilitating disease, cancer, hypertension, anxiety, diabetes.

In concluding this chapter on breath, life is breath and breath is life. As we navigate through this earth plane remembering the qualities of the soul, and joyfully living our divine self, vital breath is a necessity.

AFFIRMATION

I am inhaling love, exhaling harmony and
expanding universal vibrational frequency.

ENERGETIC
TECHNIQUES

CHAPTER 16

SOUND

In the beginning there was sound, before light. Sound is a vibration that is in the creation of the planet. "In the beginning was the Word. And the word was with God. And the word was God." John 1: 1 "The speech of men cannot reach the Lords... They must be addressed in their own language... It is composed of sounds, not words... This language, or the incantations of mantras being the most effective agent and the first of the keys which opens the door of communication between Mortals and Immortals." H. P. Blavatsky, *The Secret Doctrine*

Silence

Silence is a developing discipline to quiet one's thought, inner noise of your organs, heartbeat and sound of your breath. Silence is also where one can hear one's authentic divine voice. The silence vibration can transform into 3 psychic "Clairs;" Clairvoyance, Clairsentience and Clairaudience.

- Clairsentience is the individual high sensitivity FEELING beyond the physical plane.

- Clairaudience is the individual high sensitivity HEARING beyond the physical plane.
- Clairvoyance is the individual high sensitivity SEEING beyond the physical plane.

A Medium is a person who is psychic and also has the ability to communicate with discarnate spiritual energy. All mediums are psychic, but not all psychics are mediums.

Mantras

A mantra is sacred Sanskrit word/sound.

> *"First, God as Being. From Being comes Mind. From Mind comes Desire. From Desire comes Will. From Will comes the Word From the Word comes everything else."* – Thomas Ashley-Farrand, Healing Mantras

There are thousands of mantras but I will focus on 5 mantras in this book. A prayer can be a mantra, because it is a sound.

ONE
Aramaic translation of the Lord's Prayer of Jesus the Christ

O Birther! Father-Mother of the Cosmos, you create all that moves in light.

O Thou! The Breathing Life of all, Creator of the Shimmering Sound that touches us.

Respiration of all worlds, we hear you breathing-in and out-in silence.

Source of Sound: in the roar and the whisper, in the breeze and the whirlwind, we hear your name.

Radiant One: you shine within us, outside us-even darkness shines-when we remember.

Name of names, our small identity unravels in you, you give it back as a lesson.

Wordless Action, Silent Potency-where ears and eyes awaken, there heaven comes.

O Birther! Father-Mother of the Cosmos!

Neil Douglas-Klotz, *Prayer of the Cosmos*

TWO

The Taeeulju Mantra is a 9000-year-old mantra. The function is to return you to your original true self. I have studied this mantra for 2 ½ years as taught to me by Mr. Sechul Kim of the Jeung San Do Meditation Center. TaeeulJu Mantra is the Quintessence of the 9000-year Korean Spiritual Culture. Jeung San Do shares the teaching about the cyclic change of the Universe-Cosmic four seasons and gives you amazing experiences of Cosmic music-TaeeulJu mantra and Cosmic Dance-Dynamic meditation. TaeeulJu mantra is the mantra of finding our roots and fulfilling our wishes.

Taeeulju Mantra
Hum Chi Hum Chi
Tae eul cheon
Song won gun
Hoom ri chi ya do rac
Hoom ri ham ri sa pa ha

THREE

Aum
The primordial sound, the sound of the universe, cosmic sound.

FOUR
  Soham
  I am that, I am the divine

FIVE
  Maha-mantra
  Hare Krishna, Hare Krishna
  Krishna Krishna, Hare Hare
  Hare Rama, Hare Rama
  Rama Rama, Hare Hare

In conclusion, silent sound and breathing is the foundation of meditation. Meditation is clarifying, purifying, unifying and expands one's consciousness back to the universal consciousness of oneness. Practicing mantras daily preferable 3x a day increases your vibrational frequency facilitating your remembrance of your original divine nature.

All creation began in silence, silence to hear your inner thoughts, and thoughts are energy manifested in visible form on the physical plane.

AFFIRMATION

I am breathing and chanting divine sounds
that are unbound.

CHAPTER 17

NUTRITION/SUPPLEMENTS

Energy is needed to create life and have radiant optimal health. Deficiency of energy is noted in many medical disease, cancer and major depression. As one goes through the process of awakening to their true self requires having a surplus to energy. Therefore, it is crucial that the Body that houses the soul be honored and fed the proper nutrition, supplementation and hydrated with alkaline or reverse osmosis water.

What are the benefits of the Sun?

I strongly recommend that everyone get as much healthy rays of sun per/day. Healthy rays of sun begin at sunrise to 10am and from 3pm to sunset. It is important to drink water and sweat because vitamin D3 is made on the skin. It takes longer for individuals with darker skin to make Vitamin D3 for the sun because of the protective melanocytes. I encourage using an organic sun screen lotion because skin cancer is noted in all races. The sun produces energy for life on earth that generates heat and causes ices to melt for water flow, plant, flowers and trees to grow.

What are the benefits to Hydration?

Simply stated prolonged dehydration is the cause of death, and a host of chronic medical conditions, kidney disease, hypertension, diabetes mellitus, cancer, constipation, premature aging, decreased energy and brain fog. The body is 70% water which is a major transporter of nutrients and nerve impulses to the brain and organs for energy production for maximum function.

The regular drinking of at least eight glasses of alkaline water per day is a core foundation for enhancing your radiant health and your physical and spiritual development. One method to consider determining your maximum hydration is to measure your waist size and multiple by 2 to equal how many ounces consumed. For example, if you have a 30-inch waist (X 2), you need to consume 60 ounces of water per day. All water is not the same. Nor are they bottled the same. There are a lot of popular waters that are sold in public facilities, airports, major supermarkets, I suggest that you drink water from a glass or buy water from a BPA free products.

Some of the major benefits of drinking alkaline water is because it is an antioxidant that neutralizes free radicals. When there are more free radicals than antioxidants, this causes inflammation in your body. Inflammation is one of the causes of obesity. Ideally you want to have more antioxidants than free radicals. Free radicals are produced by digestion, by inhaling the outside fumes, using synthetic products, and pollution from vehicle exhaust and industrial pollution.

Basic Nutrition for Optimal Energetic Functioning

Nutrition is needed as we function in this physical body. There are people who are vegan, vegetarians, and carnivores, who live to be centurions with quality of life. Everyone is responsible for what they eat, and to have their own beliefs about food. I see people that does not eat anything that moves on its own be if from a religious following or personal belief. Regardless what your dietary preferences, I think your energetic thoughts affects the assimilation and vibration and frequency of the food. It is important to get your daily greens, fruits, protein, grains and fats on a daily basis. Having an attitude of gratitude, eating slowly and chewing 28 to 32 times increases digestion and metabolic energy assimilation.

Supplementation

I have found that supplement contributes to maximum energetic function:

- Vitamin C
- Vitamin D3
- Vitamin E
- Omega 3 (available in fish and vegan)
- CoQ10
- B-Complex (plant based)
- Glutathione
- L-Carnitine
- Plant based minerals
- Blue Green Algae

AFFIRMATION

I am honoring my body by drinking alkaline water
and foods daily for maximum energy.

CHAPTER 18

MOVEMENT

Be responsible for your body that encases your Godself

"Mastering the art of conscious movement is one of the best ways of keeping the life energy flowing through you-the energy that will keep you feeling young, vibrant, healthy." Dr. Jim Deaver, *The Ultimate Cure*

The ability to move is a miraculous conscious and unconscious skill. Movement includes cellular communication, nerves, bones, joint, ligaments, and muscle coordination.

Stand

One must stand before they can walk. Walking involves an awareness that I am present as my Godself and the internal soul energy. This spiritual soul DNA energy is encoded with the 4 cardinal foundational features; mobility, stability, flexibility and strength.

These four physical qualities are associated with memory awareness. For example, when you see a toddler is learning to stand there is a burning desire, relentless determination, discipline and courage. I am a fan of Yoda, a popular Star Wars Jedi teacher, who made a famous statement. **"Do. Or do not. There is no try."** (https://www.starwars.com/news/the-starwars-com-10-best-yoda-quotes) That is exactly what the toddler did to STAND.

Standing is a powerful transitional physical and spiritual milestone. Having the confidence to stand your ground is essential for living a radiant life. This confidence is also needed to speak your truth. Speaking your truth ignites remembering more of your soul qualities. Balance is needed physiologically and mentally in the transition to mobility. Living your Godself, balance is needed for the harmonious integration of the divine feminine and divine masculine.

Living a vibrant life requires movement. Regular movement and exercise are medically associated with a healthier body, sustained brain function, emotional and mental stability and managing stress to live independent as an elder effectively. There are many methods of movement I will talk about some physical movements

Walking

Walking is a safe and powerful method of moving. There are 3 types of walking that I will discuss in this book.

- *Normal walking* is the walking at a regular pace which is beneficial psychologically and physiologically that improves joint mobility, blood pressure, stress reduction, weight loss, improve lung function, leg strength and toning.

- *Power walking* is walking at more rapid pace it has the same benefit of regular walking in addition to an increase of calorie loss, lung capacity and cardiovascular leg strength and increase endurance.

- *Meditation walking* is walking at a normal pace and is used for relaxation, concentration, mental clarity and breathing with focus. An example you can practice saying your mantra when walking. You can practice breathing one step is inhaling and one step exhaling, leads to relaxation, focus and clarity of mind

Running

Running has numerous types and styles; Jogging, regular running and speed running. Running is very beneficial for your mental clarity. You connect to a euphoric feeling when you are operating in the zone. Running is associated with weight loss, to develop a higher level of coordination hands leg feet with breathing to maximize your efforts.

Swimming

Swimming is a complete exercise, beneficial for developing relaxation, toning, endurance, respiratory, cardiovascular function. Also beneficial for people with joint conditions, and difficulty walking.

Cycling

Cycling is an excellent exercise for enhancing one's neurological coordination, respiratory and cardiovascular systems, and endurance. There is a toning and strengthening of the legs and arms as well as the joints.

Sports

Volleyball, Tennis, Badminton are highly interactive sports which are beneficial in developing socialization, neurological coordination and balance. They develop creativity with improving cardiovascular and lung function.

Basketball, Football, Soccer are team sports with individuals learning to work together, socialization, coordination, and confidence. Along with the cardiovascular, respiratory and muscular benefit.

Weightlifting, Kettlebell are important for developing strength, power and resistance This is beneficial in maintaining your reproductive hormones.

Yoga is a union for your mind, body and spirit. This is beneficial for alignment, flexibility, strength and endurance.

Tai Chi Chuan is an internal martial art. It is characterized by alignment of your head and spine, relaxed chest and shoulders in coordination with one's breathing. Benefits are spiritual, physical, and medical benefits for relaxation, blood pressure, mental and emotional life.

BaQua Zhang is an internal martial art. Walking in a circle is the foundation of the style. Walking in a circle is beneficial for developing vitality, relaxation, walking meditation, spiritual unfolding and martial arts self-defense.

Boxing; Boxing is excellent for physical condition, endurance, hand and eye coordination, courage, conditioning, creativity, cardiovascular, character and sportsmanship.

Conscious movement is the bedrock of developing and maintaining radiant energy; which is needed on your journey of Joyful living of your Godself. It is a must to honor, accept and appreciate this energetic connection.

You must be responsible for your body that encases your soul.

All of the methods of movements are most effective when you workout thirty minutes per day, three times per week.

Your Movement Practice

When your movement practice is alive, it will lead you to a spiritual power that has been living dormant within you. Accessing this abundant energy will awaken the creative potential within you, and help you discover the courage needed to claim that potential.

Every breath, movement and thought becomes a way to magnetize the trillions of cells in your body and align to the multiple dimensions of your being. The result of this process is purification and a removal of all illusion, which places you in contact with your highest self. In this state you become one with the surrounding universe and your Godself, fully connected and fully aware.

When you purify, you unify. Joyfully connecting to your Godself allows you to enter a state of true friendship with the universe. This purification process consolidates and harnesses oneness with the universe. The universe reveals the incredible power within you that can be utilized to improve humanity, vibrational heart frequency and heal the abused planet earth. One's Godself is always creating ways to maximize and expand the gratitude and respect of planet Earth because there is a knowing of the interrelationship of one energy, one breath and one love of the universe.

AFFIRMATION

I am divinely moving in joy.

CHAPTER 19

AFFIRMATION SUMMARY

RECITING THE AFFIRMATION FOR MAXIMUM MANIFESTATION

1. Relax by inhaling love and exhaling harmony (3) deep breaths.

2. Smile love into your heart.

3. Select an affirmation that resonates with you AND repeat it out loud for 21 days to create a subconscious habit. Saying it throughout the day for 40 days consecutively will empower your vibrational frequency of the affirmation.

I am awakening my Soul's Love and Light shining bright for humanity's delight to be bright. Join me if you might.

I am living my soul purpose and eagerly serving humanity with my gifts.

I am totally responsible for my thoughts, beliefs, feelings, health, happiness and wealth.

I have clear thoughts of Love and Light Shining Bright.

REMEMBERING QUALITIES OF YOUR SOUL

I am receptive to living my divine true self.

I am grateful for all I have and appreciate the ability to serve.

I am creating and living my life purpose.

I am divine will living confidently and courageously.

I am Love frequency uniting energetic oneness.

I am endowed with divine courage, living day by day my joyful Godself way.

I am compassionate with myself and others.

I am beautiful and recognize beauty in all forms of life.

I am a divine servant joyfully utilizing my gifts to awaken and help others.

I am faithful in the divine process of manifesting all my goals.

I am inhaling love, exhaling harmony and expanding universal vibrational frequency.

I am breathing and chanting divine sounds that are unbound.

I am honoring my body by drinking alkaline water and foods daily for maximum energy.

I am divinely moving in joy.

CONCLUSION

Appreciate yourself for investing in remembering soul qualities. Much gratitude for allowing me to share love and light, connecting us on a universal love at truth frequency. Thanks for reading this book, to awaken, activate and allow enhancement and connectivity to *Remembering Qualities of Your Soul: Joyfully Living Your Godself.*

There are many souls that have reincarnated that are becoming aware of their inner divinity shining and sharing their unique gifts connecting with like-minded light workers. This unconditional service to humanity awakens more receptive souls creating more harmonious vibration. With the increase awakening of the one's eternal true self, it enhances purification, unification and harmonization. This is the foundation of one energy, one breath one love.

It is known that energy cannot be destroyed only transformed. Love energy is the master transformer. I am smiling Love into My Heart and transmitting to all humanity, earth and the galaxy, neutralizing frequencies of lower vibration. Remember in closing, that we all have a spiritual DNA encoded with love, light, peace, beauty, freedom, compassion, divine will, eternity and universal truth.

My soul mission is being a conduit for transmitting unconditional love and universal truth.

Let me know if I can be of more service to you.

OM SHANTI

ABOUT THE AUTHOR

Paul L. Hannah, M.D.
Master Teacher Healer

The special genius of Dr. Hannah finds expression in unique and diverse forms. From the Qi Gong classroom to remarkable one on one sessions, his holistic medical and intuitive energy awareness shines through. Dr. Hannah teaches others how to radiate love as they expand their willingness to grow and awaken their heart connection to their Soul. As a

Master Healer and Master Teacher, Paul demonstrates great love, compassion and wisdom that he shares freely with his students.

Dr. Hannah's achievements are vast and have received international recognition. He is known to be a humble lifelong student and a compassionate Master Teacher Healer, who inspires others to choose more wisely. He has transcended to his true gifts.

Dr. Hannah has studied Qi Gong with numerous masters and is an inner door disciple of Grandmaster Hong Liu. Much of his formal Qi Gong training has come from Grandmaster Hong, Grandmaster Kwok (Hong Kong), Grandmaster Wong Kiew Kit and Grandmaster T.K.Shih. On the metaphysical plane, Dr. David M. Berry introduced Dr. Hannah to the wisdom of life science and adopted him as a "spiritual son."

Professionally, Dr. Hannah is a board-certified psychiatrist and graduate of the UCLA Berkeley medical acupuncture program for physicians. He also completed training from Nanjing University, where he was licensed for acupuncture, moxibustions, and auricular therapy.

Dr. Hannah teaches others how to radiate love as they expand their willingness to grow and awaken their heart connection to their Soul. As a Master Healer/Teacher, Paul demonstrates great love, compassion and wisdom that he shares freely with his students.

Free gift on the website at this link:
https://hannahsholistichealing.com/remembering_bonus

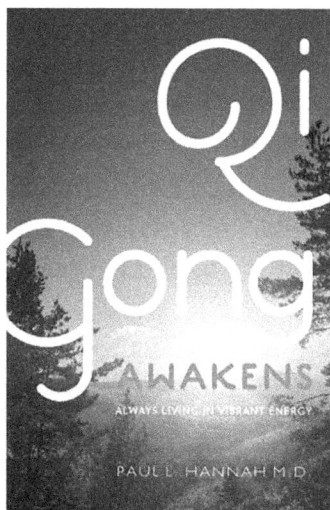

A re you ready to give yourself the gift of Vibrant Energy?

In *Qi Gong Awakens*, you will be introduced to healing breath and movements plus profound spiritual lessons

Qi Gong Awakens: Always Living in Vibrant Energy unlocks and makes accessible the wisdom of one of the most powerful of Chinese healing arts. Himself a wise physician and healer, Paul L. Hannah, MD reveals the spiritual, mental, emotional and physical principles of this ancient universal science of working with life energy. Paul L. Hannah, MD, provides a splendid effort to help integrate the principles and practice of Qi Gong with personally acquired insights into the multidimensional aspects of human existence. As a practicing psychiatrist, Paul L. Hannah, MD goes well beyond considering only the physical body and explains to the readers how to separately examine the emotional, mental and spiritual aspects of their existence. He shows how Qi Gong can help establish a functional harmony between these differing expressions of self.

The author further explains how allowing oneself to freely receive the benefits of Qi Gong helps interconnect the individual with others; leading to greater compassion, deeper understanding and a fuller appreciation of humanity. Paul L. Hannah, MD's writings describe the importance of appreciating what one can actually do now, instead of focusing on one's limitations and of embracing the opportunities for change rather than fearing having to change. These approaches provide successful formulations for ongoing progressive flow towards personal fulfillment. As a committed teacher, Paul L. Hannah, MD relates his own journey towards enlightenment to try to assist others who are receptive to his heartfelt message.

What others say about *QiGong Awakens*:

"Dr. Hannah's road in alternative medicine was similar to my path. He was one of my earliest apprentices after I arrived in the US. He learned Medicine, Psychiatry, Martial Arts and Qi Gong. He can help greatly because he sees a problem from many perspectives and can develop many solutions to the problem. I thank him for using clear English in terms from the American culture, to share Chinese Energy Medicine with the English-speaking cultures in the world." - **Grand Master Hong Liu author of Healing Arts of Qi Gong**

"Qi Gong Awakens: Always Living in Vibrant Energy *unlocks and makes accessible the wisdom of one of the most powerful of Chinese healing arts. Himself a wise physician and healer, Dr. Hannah reveals the spiritual, mental, emotional and physical principles of this ancient universal science of working with life energy. I highly recommend it to both professional and lay persons who wish to understand and practice this potent healing art."*
- **Michael Bernard Beckwith author of Life Visioning**

Purchase here:
https://hannahsholistichealing.com